I0511297

From the Academies to the Rising Sun

The Influence of Japanese Art on the Later Work of Degas and Van Gogh

By Barry De More

Copyright © 2009 by Barry De More

All rights reserved. This book or any portion thereof may not be reproduced or used in any manner whatsoever without the express written permission of the publisher except for the use of brief quotations in a book review or scholarly journal.

ISBN-13:978-1514884416
ISBN-10:1514884410

First Printing: 2009
Second Printing: 2016

- Cover Image: 'St Ives Sunrise' by Richard Walker. Available at: https://www.flickr.com/photos/richardwalkerphotography/9272644485 Under the Creative Commons Licence.

- Fig 10, Fig 28, Fig 29, Fig 30, Fig 31 © Barry De More (2009)

Printed by: Createspace

Published by: Barry De More

Website: http://barrydemoreart.weebly.com

Contact: demoreart@aol.com

CONTENTS

Acknowledgments

The author would like to thank the following people for their permission to use the following images:

All Paintings Art Portal at http://www.allpaintings.org for 'Carlo Pelligrini' by Edgar Degas

David Brooks at http://www.vggallery.com for 'Pere Tanguy' (F363, JH 1351) by Vincent Van Gogh, 'Japonaiserie: Oiran' (also known as 'The Courtesan') (F373, JH 1298) by Vincent Van Gogh, 'The Langlois Bridge with Women Washing' (F397, JH 1368) by Vincent Van Gogh, 'The Bedroom' (F484, JH1771) by Vincent Van Gogh, 'The Sower' (F451, JH 1629) by Vincent Van Gogh and 'La Crau seen from Montmajour' (F1420, JH1501) by Vincent Van Gogh

Thomas Crossland at http://www.ukiyoe-gallery.com for '100 Views of Edo – Haneda Ferry and Beteen Shrine' by Utagawa (Ando) Hiroshige

John Goulde at http://www.artgallery.sbc.edu for 'Beauty with a Letter' by Utamaro Kitagowa

Richard Kruml at http://www.japaneseprints-london.com for 'The Kintai Bridge' by Katsushika Hokusai, 'Horses in a Meadow' by Utagawa (Ando) Hiroshige and 'The Moon Pine' by Utagawa (Ando) Hiroshige

Dr Olga Mataev at http://www.abcgallery.com for 'Woman with Chrysanthemums' by Edgar Degas, 'The Bellelli Family' by Edgar Degas, 'Race Horses 1866 – 68' (Jockeys in front of the Grandstand) by Edgar Degas and 'At the Beach' by Edgar Degas

Graham Morris at http://www.battlefieldanomalies.com/solferino/index.htm for 'Napoleon III at the Battle of Solforino' by Ernest Meissonier

Wikimedia: http://www.commons.wikimedia.org for 'Olympia' by Édouard Manet, 'Le Dejeurer Sur l' Herbe' by Édouard Manet, 'The Execution of Maximillion' by Édouard Manet, 'The Bar at the Folies-Bergere' by Édouard Manet, 'Liberty Leading the People' by Eugene Delacroix, 'Stone Breakers' by Gustave Courbet, 'Young Flautist' or 'The Fifer' by Édouard Manet, 'Oiran' by Keisai Eisen and 'Ohashi Bridge in the Rain' also known as 'Evening Shower at Atake and the Great Bridge' by Utagawa (Ando) Hiroshige

Introduction

The political and cultural climate of Paris, at the time of Degas and Van Gogh, were the years after the declining power of Napoleon III and the beginning of the Third Republic which inevitably brought great changes in and around the city. Baron Haussmann at the command of Napoleon III who had grandiose ambitions for the city, demolished the historic city centre and put into operation his plan for the transformation of France and the city of Paris. Coinciding with these changes was the new direction of French art [1], in particular for those artists who desired to produce paintings based upon a more personal experience of everyday life rather than on the academies which were still quite didactic in their approach to painting and were perceived as aristocratic and rigorous. Degas was one of a number of artists who reacted against this form of strict regime.[2] For Degas and other like-minded French painters, who had not yet formulated their own style of working in a contemporary vein, the Japanese Ukiyo-e was to prove of important value. French artists were thus able to inform and incorporate Japanese elements of the Japanese woodblock prints into their own work, in combination with the study of their environment, interests and observations. [3]

In analysing Degas and Van Gogh's work it is important to discover how the changes in Paris caused the new direction in 19th Century French art. For example, before 1848 narrow streets and bridges encumber the city until the middle of the 19th Century, by which time the whole city had gone through a massive building project. Whole districts were razed to the ground to make way for the new tree lined boulevards, countless opera houses, theatres and café concerts. By the 1870s hundreds of miles of streets had been altered to fit in with the modern boulevards and the newly transformed city of Paris. [4]

Due to these economic and cultural changes a 'new' kind of art began to emerge by artists representing these changes in their paintings, for example, Monet, Manet, Degas, Renoir, Morissot and Cassett, whose interest lay in depicting contemporary life. This was to a degree, the birth of Modernism. Modernism refers to artists and individual artistic movements which arose in the first half of the 20th Century. From its beginnings it was a deliberate challenge against the accepted traditional values of representation.[4a] At this time France also became a sparkling centre for tourism and commerce. Trade relations between France and Japan opened up subsequently allowing Japanese art to begin flowing into France. [5] Exotic and entrancing Japanese artwork could be found in many shops in Paris. The prints of the Ukiyo-e artists were most popular with the artists of Paris during the mid and late 19th Century[6] and the word "Japonisme" coined by the French critic Philip Burty was the term used for the study of Japanese culture and aesthetics by artists and writers after Burty realised that the craze for everything Japanese was having a tremendous influence on the visual arts in various ways, in particular among the painters in Paris.[7]

The following analysis will, therefore, examine how Edgar Degas and Vincent Van Gogh were influenced by this Japanese art with specific reference to the Ukiyo-e. I will also analyse a number of works by both artists, and make a more in depth study of Degas' "Jockeys in Front of the Grandstand" (1869-72) and Van Gogh's "Drawbridge with Carriage" (1888). In chapter two I will investigate some of the main causes of the birth of Modernism to consider its influence on these artists. I will conclude by outlining some of the similarities between Degas and Van Gogh's practice and my own practice.

In Pursuit of Modernity

My analysis begins with one of Degas' earliest works "Woman with Chrysanthemums" (1865), Fig 1, here he has clearly demonstrated the use of Japanese composition. See, for example, the print by Utamaro Kitagowa (1750-1806) "Beauty with a Letter", Fig 2. In his pursuit of a modern type, it can be seen that Degas has moved away from the conventional composition seen in Fig 3.[8] In Fig 1 the sitter Madam Hertel stares, as if in a daydream, out of the picture to the right; and the whole scene is dominated by the large vase of flowers, which is viewed from a slightly high angled viewpoint. Evidently, at least two features point directly to the influence of Japan. Firstly, the major subject has been decentralised, which is Degas' first use of asymmetrical composition. The second feature is the unusual use of viewpoint. This device was used to view the subjects in interesting flat shapes, but with edges clearly defined. [9]

Another concept in Japanese art is the transition from background to foreground or middle distance which appears quite abrupt. This idea is seen in "The Beach Scene", Fig 4. It is clear that the space in this painting is uncertain, maybe revealing a less confident Degas of the 1860s. This oil on canvas produced in 1876 depicts figures in the foreground surrounded with all their paraphernalia and appear to float in mid-air. The space occupied seems quite different from that where the figures are on the shoreline and in the sea. As Whitford points out, it is possible that Degas had not yet quite learnt or absorbed the lessons of Japanese aesthetics.[10] Initially Degas demonstrated boundless admiration for Ingres, only mentioning Japanese prints once in his correspondences. Nevertheless Degas, according to Whitford, believed that the use of Japanese prints, for their compositional devices, would help to refine his style. The Ukiyo-e subjects were also the same as those he desired to represent in his own paintings.[11]

What the Japanese prints offered artists such as Degas, and for that matter his close friend Manet and other French painters, was not the exotic subjects. On the contrary, seemingly they were chosen for their depiction of everyday urban life which Degas and Manet may have preferred in place of the didactic, conventional, idealised subjects prescribed by the academies. This resulted during the 1840s and 50s with an increase in the painting of landscape and rural civilization, and in the 1860s a growing interest and preoccupation with depicting the contemporary urban arena. Manet was the forerunner of the latter trend, during the daytime he explored various themes such as parks and boulevards and in the evening opera and the ballet. Two paintings executed by Manet portray his new interest in modern urban imagery "Luncheon on the Grass", Fig 5, and "Olympia", Fig 6. These two examples demonstrate how Manet suggested modern life more directly to the viewer. It was around the 1860s that Manet and Degas met. They had similar interests in cosmopolitan subjects and would therefore encourage one another in finding new themes to portray; specifically it was at the racetrack where both artists' interests met.[11a] Moreover, what they perceived in the Ukiyo-e woodblocks was a new and refreshing aesthetic.[12] Degas began turning away from the aristocratic symbolism of the academies and, through the Japanese influence, was inspired to transpose traditional motifs into a contemporary realistic context.[13]

Another important way in which the Ukiyo-e prints helped to bring about changes in French art was that Ukiyo-e artists such as Suzuki Horunobu (1727-1770), Utamaro Kitagowa (1750-1806), Utagowa (Ando) Hiroshige

(1797-1858), Hokusai Katsushika (1760-1848) and Eise Ikedo (1790-1848) produced popular images that distinguished Japanese art from the exclusive art of the aristocratic court. For the Ukiyo-e artist this was a period of new consciousness in depicting the world as they saw it, and not being bound by the decadent feudal system. This then was an area which the French painters of the 19th Century felt they held in common with Ukiyo-e artists.[14]

Degas' painting "Carlo Pellegrini" (1876-77), Fig 7, exhibits further ideas associated with Japanese aesthetics and traits. For example, the figure of the subject is depicted in a characteristic pose, the shape of which is in solid mass of almost dark tonal values. He is viewed from a high angle, which in turn gives the illusion of the ground on which he stands being brought up close to the picture plane.[15] The Japanese design factors are seen when compared with Hiroshige's print of "Horses in a Meadow", Fig 8.[16]

In like manner "Race Horses 1866-68" also known as "Jockeys in Front of the Grandstand", Fig 9, appears to have been influenced by Japanese prints. The forms have been suggested with clear and skilful outline, the modelling has been kept to a minimum and the paint has been laid down in flat swatches. [17] Degas also uses off-centre positioning known as 'asymmetry', learnt from the Ukiyo-e. Moreover, the large void area in the centre of the painting, a Japanese technique, uses space in a positive manner, instead of the Western tradition of box perspective. Using flat areas of space not only suggests a surface that is receding and creates a sense of depth in the picture plane, but also acts as a counterbalance in its sheer simplicity.[18] Empty spaces were regarded by the Japanese printmakers as active areas and not negative and were considered as important as the other components in the composition. By all accounts this compositional device, the most important one in Japanese prints, is exactly what Degas incorporates into his painting.[19]

During research I have been intrigued to discover in "Jockeys in Front of the Grandstand" close similarities between the horse at the apex of the triangle – on which the composition is based, and which is bolting – and the horse depicted by Hokusai, Fig 10. (Fig 10 is my copy after Hokusai as I could not locate the copyright holder for permission to publish). On occasions Degas used the camera to inform his work, but it is possible that in this case the source, as Whitford suggests, could have come from Hokusai's Manga whose study was produced without the use of photography, on all accounts.[20] Because Degas' image is so closely similar to Hokusai's horse, it seems reasonable to suggest that Degas informed his work through the study of Japanese images and aesthetics.[21]

Regarding whether or not this painting has been wholly influenced by Japanese art, it would appear not if, according to Reff's suggestions, the two foreground horses in the painting have derived from a picture by Meissonier (1815-89), Fig 11, titled "Napoleon III at the Battle of Solferino" (1859).[22] Here clear similarities can be seen in Meissonier's horses, and those depicted in "Jockeys in Front of the Grandstand". Although Degas' interest in the horse was stimulated by the work of Theodore Gerecault (1791-1824), he additionally informed his work from sporting prints from England. Moreover, the Japanese compositional device of silhouette is seen in this painting because the features of the horses and riders are not clearly defined, but are in silhouette. Degas wrote from New Orleans "And then I love silhouette so much..." [23]

A clear demonstration of Japanese art can also be seen in the truncation of the horse in the foreground and the grandstand. However, there is also the illusion of Western ideas of perspective. So, in this painting Degas appears to be using a mix of Western and Japanese aesthetics. The painting, executed with a limited palette but with precision, and painted with flat paint, is again a Japanese influence. Degas used line to model his subject more than with paint. Patches of red indicated in the mounts and figures in the crowd carry extra warmth and harmony and balance through the painting, adding to the appearance of a bright summer's day, as these are complementary to the greens. And the luminosity of the light effect is brought about by the strong contrasting tonal values of the shadows and the complementary value of the ground.

The painting is of an ordinary everyday scene, possibly because by now Degas was familiar with the Café Guerbois and associated with the artists who were to become known as the Impressionists after 1874. They met together to discuss poetry, music and art, and it was not long before Degas' art began to illustrate his changing ideas towards contemporary art. In the latter half of the 1860s, giving up his former paintings of historical genre, he turned to new inspiration found at the racetrack which was also newly developed due to the transformation that had taken place in France, under the leadership of Haussmann when modernising the city.[24]

Degas had a desire to explore his theories of modernity and was unbiased in his attitude toward permissible subject matter.[25] It was now Degas' response to the real and the actual, as he saw it, that would satisfy his appetite for a more contemporary working out of his subject matter. He became more interested in the behaviour of the figure and the seemingly trivial detail.[26]

Turning my attention to Vincent Van Gogh and the influence of Japanese art on his work, it was while in Paris that he collected for the first time huge amounts of Japanese prints; as did many other Impressionists. The first painting under discussion is of his friend Pere Tanguy who is sat against a backdrop of Japanese prints, Fig 12. The original prints are by Hokusai, Hiroshige and Eisen. In this painting Van Gogh's enthusiasm for Impressionism is noticeable, as well as the vivacity described in the use of his brushstrokes, because he had not yet assimilated Japanese aesthetics. What is significant in his process of assimilation is that between 1887 and 1889 he produced copies in oil of Japanese woodcut prints from a series called *One Hundred Views of Edo* by Hiroshige. "The Ohashi Bridge in the Rain", No. 52, (1857), Fig 13, is an example from this series.

Japanese art and culture played an important role in the development of Van Gogh's art and may have been a lifelong influence.[27] He not only copied their motifs but also as an avid collector of Japanese Ukiyo-e he would at times add symbols from other Japanese prints and incorporate these into the composition. For example, the painting "Courtesan", Fig 14, was from an original print by Keisai Eisen (1790-1848), Fig 15. The frogs in the painting are copied from Yoshimaru's "New Prints of Insects", and the stork in the picture is from "Geisha in Landscape" by Sato Torakiyo. Apart from this painting, Van Gogh also copied "Plum Garden at Kameido" by Hiroshige, and "Ohashi Bridge in the Rain" – two prints in the book *One Hundred Views of Edo.*[28] The painting "Courtesan" was also directly influenced by the French magazine "Paris Ilustre", volume 4, May 1886, which was devoted entirely to Japan and described its culture, history, climate, customs, education, religion, visual arts and the character of its people.[29]

Van Gogh's working method, while in Paris, was to assimilate from the influences around him; in addition to incorporating influences from the Japanese prints. For him it was a search for, or to formulate his own artistic idiom. His work also drew from the Impressionists' values. The Japanese concepts of aesthetics were often practised by the Impressionists. One of these techniques was the truncation of forms, but critics and painters from the old school expressed their disgust and shock. These included Charles Gleyre (1804-1874), Alexander Cabinel (1823-1888) and Franz von Lenbach (1836-1904) who said, "The Impressionist – these croppers – off of necks and heads – despise the close form of the human body which have been taught to us by the Old Masters".[30] Nevertheless Van Gogh chose to paint the same subject matter as his contemporaries, his palette becomes a lot lighter and he soon begins to use the techniques of Neo-Impressionism. Van Gogh also begins to experiment with colour in a way that was new to him. He wrote, "What is required in art nowadays is something very much alive, very strong in colour, very much intensified".[31]

Van Gogh was determined to understand the complexities of using colour and his experimentation with colour harmonies and contrasts came about because of his interest in Impressionism, Neo-Impressionism and the Japanese print. For Van Gogh, these experiments and exercises proved worthwhile. He later wrote to his sister, "And when I painted the landscape in Asnieves this summer, I saw more colour there than ever before".[32]

The painting of "The Langlois Bridge", also known as the "Drawbridge with Carriage", Fig 16, also demonstrates some degree of Japanese influence, especially with the use of varying colour combinations. It was executed while in Arles, Southern France, and was among his first works after soon arriving there. Van Gogh wrote to his brother Theo on March 10th 1888 about this:

> I brought back a Number 15 square canvas today. The subject is a drawbridge with a small vehicle crossing it, outlined against a blue sky, the stream being also blue, the banks orange with some green. There is a group of washer-women in blouses and brightly coloured headdresses.[33]

The painting expresses a sunny time of day and the air appears to be clear. The subjects are clearly defined and precisely outlined, suggestive of one of the Ukiyo-e methods.[34] The subject of the painting itself is Japanese: bridges were admired by the Ukiyo-e artists, firstly for their engineering and carpentry techniques, and secondly for their role as landmarks. Also Van Gogh uses the Japanese device of flattened perspective throughout the composition. Then there are, of course, the colours which are uniformly bright and pure, the outlines are also sharp and precise.[35] Van Gogh, however, was not trying to engage in the same principles as the Impressionists in the suggestion of depicting light effect because this area of their work excessively subdued the detail in drawing, and for Van Gogh this limited the process of describing the image.[36]

Van Gogh's work here in Arles is totally different from those produced in Paris. For example, he was now inspired by the strange appearance of light and colour, and was beginning to produce paintings in an individualistic approach, using his own language in the use of paint and colour. Whereas his time working in Paris, experimenting in colour and various other techniques, meant that he was creating a body of work which was not consistent in its approach to painting. Nevertheless, he learnt a great deal from the Impressionists, and once in Arles he became surer of his own language of personal response.[37]

Regarding the colour in "The Langlois Bridge", this is intensified to the same degree of saturation throughout the painting. The area of space in the water at the right is not negative space, but an area that counterbalances the left hand side of the painting occupied by the busy washer-woman, the half-sunken boat and the banking. This is a Japanese device. The clarity, approach and animation in the painting are also direct influences of the Japanese Ukiyo-e artists. This is clearly demonstrated in Van Gogh's economical and abbreviated rendering of the subject. Also, he uses colour in a way that does not reflect the literal scene before him but he demonstrates through colour his own personal language and response to the subject.

Van Gogh's script in this painting has numerous variations. In the poplars there are short thin strokes, broader and larger strokes in the water, cross-hatching in the water in dark blue which emphasises the reflection of the bridge; and swirling gestural strokes describe the ripples in the water where the women wash their clothes. The bridge is painted with various sizes of rectangles, squares and dabs that register as stones. In the orange bank on the left there are short dabs and strokes. Evidently, therefore, Van Gogh produced a painting that is very Japanese in its composition, motif, use of space, use of colour, clarity and rendering of animation.

Arles was Japan for Vincent Van Gogh.[38] Writing to his sister he stated:

> I don't need any Japanese prints because I always say that I am in Japan right here. And that I therefore only have to open my eyes and paint whatever is in front of my nose and makes an impression on me.[39]

Though these impressions were not the kind experienced by Pissarro or Monet. Van Gogh's impressions, to which he dedicated himself enthusiastically, were about recording the overall visual impact and response.[40] With this aim in mind he produced "The Drawbridge with Carriage".[41]

Referring to the way that Van Gogh used colour in this painting, and in others while in Arles, he has said "I have used colour more arbitrary in order to express myself forcibly". Pissarro (1830-1903), one of Van Gogh's contemporaries, no doubt understood his meaning as it was Pissarro who encouraged artists "to exaggerate boldly the effects of either harmony or discord which colour produces".[42] Van Gogh, then, is able to express the southern summer.[43]

Yet another clear example of how he uses colour in an expressive way to suggest emotion is his painting of the bedroom, Fig 17. He employs areas of uniform flat colours, again illustrating the Ukiyo-e influence, of complementary orange and blue, violet and yellow, red and green. In a letter to Paul Gauguin he explains what this colour scheme denotes, "I wanted all these different colours to express a totally restful feeling".[44]

A further instance in which Van Gogh was influenced by Japanese art is evident in the painting entitled "The Sower", Fig 18, which derives from a painting by Jean Francois Millet (1814-75). The influence is instantly recognizable in the flattening of the composition, as can be seen in Hokusai's print of "Bridge with Five Arches", also known as "The Kintai Bridge", Fig 19. The large disc portraying the sun and the tree that cuts through the picture plane at a very acute angle is also Japanese, see Fig 20. The use of a strong foreground object, in this case the rower (Fig 21) is used to create the illusion of depth, pushing back the picture space, and is known as repoussoir.[45] The painting was a challenge to Van Gogh in that he desired to produce an original piece of contemporary art, since studying in Paris. Thus it is the very bold palette and the juxtaposed colour on which the originality is based.[46]

In "The Sower" the colours are predominantly bolder than in "The Langlois Bridge with Women Washing". They are also discordant and harmonic to produce a painting of bravura, and the pigments used are not over dramatic in emphasising the suggestion of the setting sun. There is the close relationship between the intensities of values in the depiction of the sky and the land mass, in producing a balanced harmony throughout the painting. The green that is produced in the sky is echoed in the figure of the sower and in the fields and tree. Van Gogh carries this colour around the canvas creating yet again harmonious continuity as in the disc of the sun. The dark edge of the tree and again the figure are the influence of the Ukiyo-e print. Strong contrasting in this way makes the painting a powerful image.

Moreover, the application of the paint is varied in that Van Gogh uses his own personal language of marks produced with the brush. This language also derived from and was influenced by the Japanese artists.

As already stated, Van Gogh did not go to the extremes of using these penetrating expanses of flat areas, but instead devised a graphic metaphor of personal language. When first looking at the influence of Japanese art in Van Gogh's work, it may appear that he is working in a totally contrasting manner, when in fact it is a direct Japanese source. For example, when looking at illustrations in books by Ukiyo-e artists, they were sometimes produced in colour, but more often than not in black and white. For these they explored various techniques for rendering textures, and patterns for distinguishing different areas. These effects can be seen in the work of Hiroshige Fig 8, and an example of this Japanese device is clearly evident in Van Gogh's "La Crau", Fig 22 (1888) using pen and ink with a variety of reed pens in various widths.[47]

In "The Sower" this varied language of marks, inspired by the Ukiyo-e print makers[48], can be seen in the area of the sky on the right which has been painted with brushstrokes that are more or less horizontal. To the left of the sun the brush marks follow the form of the sun in short strokes, the sun also is depicted in a similar rhythm. The modern look of the painting comes about clearly through the statement of bold colour and, in my opinion, gives a sense of quietness and calm. Van Gogh, then, influenced by Japanese print executed his first piece of contemporary art.

From Ancient to Modern

Singularity, that is individualism, has been the 'norm' since Romanticism was established in the 19th Century, and this is the touchstone of Modernism, and it has never established a style of its own. The principles of Modernism have been autonomy and freedom for individuals, freedom from skilled knowledge and mastery of techniques, freedom from didactic regimes and of tradition and academies, according to Goblik.[49]

It is possible, however, that the roots of Modernism stem further back into history than the 19th Century, according to Witco. It seems that the Renaissance is the period that Modernism began. It is at this time when secular humanism is encountered. This is the idea that man (not God) is the measure of all things. In these humanist ideas, which desired a more perfect society[50], a worldly civic consciousness and 'Utopia' were the Modernist way of thinking which emerged in the Renaissance and which really began to take shape in the 18th Century.[51] I will briefly make mention of the 'Ancient' and 'Moderns' and their differences as this is relevant to the argument concerning why Degas and Van Gogh and other 19th Century artists for that matter painted how they painted and what they painted.

There is what is known as the "Quarrel of the Ancients and Moderns" this was an ongoing dispute that dominated intellectual life through the century.[52] At the roots of this quarrel were the Moderns, those living in the 18th Century who considered themselves more superior than the Ancients in morals and artistically. The Ancients were the Greeks and Romans. Those who tended to support the argument for the Ancients were the conservative forces, and the progressive forces supported the Moderns.[53] Without going into the subject too deeply, I shall outline who the Ancients and Moderns were in simple terms.

The Ancients after the revolution of 1789 were to be identified with the old order of the ancient regime, and the Moderns were concerned with the movement called romanticism. These two movements then had their own vision of the future and were soon politicized. The Ancients in their thinking and beliefs were politically conservative and were connected with classicising academic art. The Moderns were seen as revolutionary and progressive left wing and linked with anti-academic Romanticism. This division can be seen in the rivalry between Eugene Delacroix (1798-1863) and Jean-Auguste-Dominique Ingres (1780-1867). The two artists exhibited in the Salon of 1824. Ingres exhibited his "Vow of Louis XIII" and Delaciox "The Massacre of Scios". Ingres' painting was academically correct and classical in its theme. Its values in the ancient regime represented the good old days of the ancient order and tradition; whereas the Moderns, which were politically progressive, saw in the painting of Delacroix an artist who was representative of revolution, anarchy and of intellectuals. The subject matter in his painting was connected with materialism and modern or contemporary life, and was viewed as ugly by the Ancients.[54]

It appears that progressive Modernism extends from Delacroix to Gustave Courbet (1819-1877) and Manet (1832-1883). From the Ancients' point of view Delacroix's Romanticism, Manet's Naturalism and Courbet's Realism were considered cults of ugliness that rebelled against academic ideals of what was termed beautiful.[55]

The progressive Modernists continually concerned themselves with depicting in their paintings contemporary life. Also in this group there were a number of artists who continued to focus their attention in their pictures on the social and political dilemmas of contemporary society either directly or indirectly.[56] For example, I can see in Delacroix's painting "Liberty Leading the People", Fig 23, his apparent support for the revolution of 1830. And again Courbet demonstrates a socialist statement in the picture "The Stone Breakers", Fig 24, and then there is Manet who makes his political painting of "The Execution of Maximilion", Fig 25.[57] Progressive Modernism then by the 19th Century sought to exercise artistic freedom. This was not simply from the strict regime of the didactic academies but also from the demands of the public.[58] So then, during this age of Modernism that grew out of 19th Century France 'traditional' literature and forms of art had now become 'old fashioned' it would therefore be more beneficial and essential if these Modernist ideas were to develop, to push the deeply grounded traditions to one side and begin afresh.[59]

Modernism is closely related to Modern Art, but Modernism relates from the "then" of the late 19th Century to the onset of the 1970s. During this period artists began experimenting with various ideas of seeing; these artists were seeking a 'new' approach to how they as individuals could depict the world around them. It was no longer important to represent a subject in a realistic manner. Due to the developments in photography these ideas had become obsolete. It was then the new approach to explore different media, materials, nature and the whole function of art.[60]

One idea of the modern movement was to re-evaluate the present cultural system by discovering what was 'holding back' progress and to readjust by replacing it with new ideas. People were encouraged to accept these new ideas, and to change their world view because the new, they said, was good and beautiful.[61]

Even so not everyone agreed with the new ideas of the Modernist's doctrines. Some continued in the classical school of thought and then of course there was the revolutionist movement for example the Pre-Raphaelite Brotherhood. There were also a number of writers such as John Ruskin (1819-1900) and anti-rationalist philosopher Hegel (1770-1831). These and other reactionists together seemed to challenge any ideas of certainty and stability either derived by pure reason or civilization.[62] In addition to the above, the eastern decorative arts that flooded into France became an important area of influence among many artists, the main influence being the Japanese prints, and in particular the Ukiyo-e.[63]

Also it is important to mention the fact that the French Revolution provided the driving force so to speak, for the avant-garde culture that did not conform to the traditional academic authority that had absolute command and control over the art market, now these artists could be individuals, standing on his/her own feet.[64] Avant-garde is a term given to describe progressive innovators, especially in the arts. [64a]

A major factor that brought about dramatic changes in 19th Century French art was the transformation of the old city into a new modern metropolis of commerce and tourism which was touched on earlier. The new boulevards served as the most important space for the French capital. For Paris at the 1867 Universal Exhibition it was a celebration of the newly transformed city into a modern international capital. And this modern city was of great interest for a group of avant-garde painters who claimed to be modern, specifically Monet, Renoir (1841-1919) and

Manet. These artists painted the busy urban arena and other areas of the city, namely the gardens and parks. So a newly designed city brought about a different kind of painting by France's contemporary artists.[65]

Coinciding with these changes was the Industrial Revolution which also brought a new and materialistic lifestyle for Parisians. With its new rail links and huge steel bridges making way for larger shipping to transport goods further up the Seine travelling for work or pleasure became easier for all social classes as travel became more affordable to the populous. The city and suburbs became an ideal place for a new kind of art.[66]

As well as the above being an inspiration for painting there were also the very popular cafés that became extremely fashionable towards the mid-19th Century in Paris and the suburbs. Such cafés as the Café Guerbois, the café concerts or cabarets and the Le Moulin de la Gallet were all popular themes for some of these modern artists who wanted to suggest the lure of these establishments and to depict contemporary life which was frowned upon by the academies.[67]

The spirit of modern life in Paris can be clearly seen in the painting by the French painter Édouard Manet "A Bar at the Folies-Bergere", Fig 26, which engages us, in a sense, and demonstrates in part contemporary life in the 20th Century. The imagery depicts a great deal of Paris for which the city was famous. The huge chandelier may signify the glamour of Paris, and from the reflection in the mirror, it appears to be a large ballroom. There is the woman in the background who is focused on the circus suggested by the trapeze artist at the top left. This, then, is one scene of nightlife in Paris: crowds of people drinking and enjoying the entertainment, all part of the new Paris built by Haussmann[68], and conveying the idea of the modern culture of Paris.[69]

Equally important in the search for producing a contemporary painting was the use of photography. This development revolutionised the way that painters saw the world. Degas and others were acquainted with the photographer Felix Nadar and, apparently, the first Impressionist Exhibition was held at the photographer's home. Photography for the artist was useful in the study of light and movement.[70]

In addition to the aid of photographs there was also the influence of the Japanese Ukiyo-e woodblock prints. Ukiyo-e means pictures of the Floating World and the Ukiyo-e artists based their themes on the variations of life as a transient experience.[71] These prints only became available because in 1853 Commodore Matthew C Perry went to Japan; the country had closed its doors to Europe for the last 125 years, apart from with the Dutch who had some trade relations with them. Once Japan was opened there was a tremendous influx of exotic Japanese goods exported to Europe.[72] In 1882 the shop La Porte Chinoise opened in Paris which then became the main supply of imported goods from the east, and was frequented by artists and critics alike. This then was the beginning of the craze for everything Japanese. It was not long before artists became collectors of Japanese objects and incorporated them as props into their paintings. Monet uses the kimono in his painting "La Japonaise", Manet a decorative fan in "Lady with a Fan", then there is his painting of "Emile Zola" that incorporates a folding screen and woodblock prints.

Apart from the aforementioned props there was also the influence of the Japanese woodblock prints. It was from these prints that artists were able to study and become aware of what could be more beneficial to them, in relation to the aesthetic behind the prints. Therefore by adopting Japanese compositional devices into their work they were beginning to produce modern imagery. This is known as "Japonisme" as opposed to "Japonaiserie" which is simply using Japanese props in a picture.[73]

In addition to this there was also the World's Fair of 1867. Artists would have no doubt attended and viewed oriental art and prints and realized that there was potential in these, as it were, to give a new animation to their imagery, as they analysed Japanese motifs and concepts.[74]

One of these concepts of compositional devices is truncation of forms. This idea can be seen in Japanese screens. The diptychs demonstrate how this idea of cropping may have come about. The forms on Japanese screens were cut off by one panel and continued on the next panel. The Ukiyo-e printmakers realised that not only did this process of truncation add visual excitement but it added a sense of depth also, consequently adapting this idea into a single print.[75]

A further compositional device is asymmetry which was also used by Degas in his painting 'Woman with Chrysanthemums'. Asymmetry is when one side of the composition is not in balance with the other, but both parts are organised in such a way that there is a compositional harmony. This use of asymmetry is a characteristic of the Japanese Ukiyo-e and this intentional difference is called 'hacho'.[76]

The Impressionists, therefore, may have incorporated new Japanese aesthetics into their work as a means of breaking out of the old traditions. The woodblock prints depicted images of a life of pleasure, theatres, courtesans and actors. The most prominent leading figures were notably Utagawa (Ando) Hiroshige (1797-1853), Katsushika Hokusai (1760-1849) and Kitagowa Utamaro (1753-1806). These prints were admired and collected by the Impressionists who were now keen on painting the modern city and its daily life which was no doubt new and challenging.[77]

The Impressionists responded with enthusiasm to these prints because they struck a chord with the forward looking artists of Paris. The Impressionists were rooted in modernity; and the images of the woodblock prints provided a new range of luxurious ideas.[78] As a consequence Japanese art seemed to provide a new alternative to the established tradition of European art.[79] With the arrival of Modernism many artists were breaking away from the classicized academic art with its traditions of methodology. Though it appears quite contradictory, the fact is that the art that had become so influential was itself saturated in strict tradition; alternatively to these French painters Japanese art appeared as a breakthrough, they could now adopt Japanese aesthetics of composition and form.[80]

Furthermore what the Japanese prints had to offer the new modern artist was not only confirmation of their own ideas, but also provided new visual answers for solving old problems of representing form. Artists could also see what effectual visual achievements could be achieved by placing their subjects off-centre, and at times cropping off part of the subject with the edge of the picture frame. Similarly with the developments in photography, and Japonisme, there was a new interest in the arrangement of composition in perspective and also the use of space that created interest with the artists who incorporated similar ideas into their paintings. What many artists achieved with these new concepts was a suggestion of a momentary quality; they were exploring and considering new aesthetic principles, which may largely have been triggered by Japanese art.[81]

Furthermore, up until the 19th Century optical representation had been the norm and tradition in European art, the technique had been developed in Greece. Artists and architects of the early Renaissance developed these ideas of optical representation even further and discovered linear perspective. It was the marriage of optics and geometry that now enabled artists to suggest a pictorial space. Again it was the artist of the Renaissance who perfectly understood the technique of Chiaroscuro, the illusion of light and shadow, which had been the traditions of the academies.[82]

However, Jan Krikke stated in his paper "China, Japan and the Birth of Modernism" that the major role for the development of the Modernist revolution was due in part to the artistic culture of China and that Japan was the intermediary, and that China gave to this movement the fundamental principles in architecture and art.[83] Japanese Ukiyo-e prints used very different compositional devices, and linear perspective was not one of them. They used the projection method devised by Chinese artists; this is known as axonometry or "parallel perspective". Furthermore and as stated previously the Japanese woodblock printers produced images in flat areas of colour, and as there is no light source there is therefore no shadow.[84]

An example of incorporating Japanese elements into his paintings, apart from the two main characters mentioned, was Édouard Manet in his painting "The Fifer" (1866), Fig 27, which is painted in flat unmodulated colours and with very little modelling in clair-obscure (clair-obscure is the French translation of the Italian chiaroscuro). The critics were outraged calling him "a painter of playing cards", but Manet it seems became the hero of like-minded modern artists of the time such as Renoir, Pissarro, and Monet[85] who were similarly influenced by Japanese art. The critic Edmond de Goncourt (1822-96) pointed out the Japanese role of the modernisation of European painting:

> When I said that Japonism was in the process of revolutionising the vision of the European people, I meant that Japonism brought to Europe a new sense of colour, a new decorative system, and if you will, a poetic imagination in the invention of the objet d'art, which never existed even in the most perfect medieval or Renaissance pieces." [86]

The arrival of modern art becomes apparent also when comparing it with the art of the academies. For example, the Old Masters believed in the importance of the presence of the flatness of the picture plane and were able to produce vivid illusions of three dimensional space on this flatness. The viewer only becomes aware of the flatness of the picture after seeing what is 'in' the painting. Whereas in a Modernist painting the picture – the flatness – is seen first and what the flatness contains is seen next. Arguably, this is the only way of seeing a picture, either Old Master or Modernist, though the Modernist would propose that it is the necessary and only way. [87]

The sheer frankness of Manet's painting is an example which openly declares the flat painting surface, as in the Japanese prints, and singles him out as a Modernist who viewed the flat surface as positive. This was in contrast to the Old Masters who viewed the surface as negative, and who have been described as illusionists employing art to hide art; the Modernist however sought to bring attention to it. For example, the Old Masters regarded the limitations of the medium of painting such as the shape of the support, the flat surface and the properties of the pigment as negative. The Modernists on the other hand regarded these limitations as positive, openly displaying the surface on which they painted. [88]

Moreover, the Impressionists who followed Manet abandoned techniques such as underpainting and glazing to leave the viewer in no doubt that real colour was employed from real pots of paint. Also, Paul Cézanne sometimes created designs to fit more comfortably into the rectangular shape of the canvas, as though this process sacrificed verisimilitude.[89] Therefore, turning away from the literal representation of the subject, Cézanne was determined to produce contemporary paintings whereby his attempts appear to transpose his private sensations into the paintings, as did Van Gogh; and if the final image was uncouth and abrasive it was because Cézanne could be all of these things. [90] Cézanne had his own independent vision of expression [91] and his interest in colour, and with nature itself, presented the greatest difficulties, but which he aimed to treat in a highly individual way. [92]

In addition to this, Cézanne shared with the Impressionists the portrayal of the landscape. His brushwork was a variation of the brushwork of artists like Monet and Pissarro; although Cézanne's use of brush is of a more orderly principle placed down in mosaic-like blocks of verticals and diagonals, which emphasise the rhythm of the landscape and structure of the finished piece – thus rendering his sensations of natural living forms. Whether painting portraits, still life or landscapes, these provided the essential theme for his work. [93]

Picasso once insisted that it was Cézanne's anxiety that impressed him above all. His contemporary Matisse, writing concerning a small painting which he owned by Cézanne, said that it had "sustained me spiritually in the critical moments of my career as an artist". Cézanne's dramatic use of colour, his concern with geometry and how he constructs his paintings evidently influenced his contemporaries. [94]

In Modernism, it was the flatness of the support that remained fundamental in the process, and which critically defined Modernism in pictorial art. The flatness was unique to that art. [95] That is not to say that Modernist painting turned its back on the representation of the subject, but what it did abandon in principle was the recognisable three dimensional space of the subject, that is, what the object inhabited. [96]

Because of its autonomy and desire to break away from the literary mimetic depiction or representation, Modernist painting broke away from anything it may have had in common with sculpture. In other words, the Modernist renounced three dimensionality in the belief that this area belonged to sculpture. The painter David (1748-1825) however sought to revive sculptural three dimensional representation in painting to try and save pictorial art from the flattening out of the picture plane induced by emphasising colour.[97]

As documented previously, in the beginning of the Modernist era, the Modernists were influenced in part by oriental aesthetics, in particular the Japanese Ukiyo-e prints. In seeking to depict contemporary art the modern Impressionists were even against modelling in shade to suggest form, and for that matter anything else that seemed to connote the sculptural. [98] In their search for a 'new' kind of contemporary painting, Manet and the Impressionists seemed to undermine everything that suggested the sculptural. Likewise, Cézanne and the Cubists in their driving search for originality followed on. The Cubist reaction against the Impressionists brought about a painting that was flatter than had probably been produced in Western art, at least before Cimabue (1240-1302). [99] The Modernist artistic aims were above all else individuality. [100]

The Impressionists including Degas and Van Gogh, although they were not Impressionists in the real sense of the word, had made a break from the academy's institutionalised teachings. But most of all, they broke away from naturalism, both romantic and photographic, which at the time was the only accepted theory considered worthy in this era of democracy and developing science. [101] The first Post-Impressionist exhibition was the work of a number of artists endeavouring to produce paintings in a pictorial language appropriate to their personal response to the modern outlook. [102] The Modernistic pursuit was not to produce descriptive images of natural forms. On the contrary, they sought to create a new form of language which they felt was equivalent of life. Henry Matisse, for example, with the influence of oriental artists was able to demonstrate convincingly in his work the objects that stimulated his creative desires. He transposed this subject into an equivalent through the use of special relationships, line and particularly colour. [103] I would suggest that Matisse's painting "The Dessert, Harmony in Red" (1908) is influenced by the Japanese Ukiyo-e because of the decorative design, the bold use of colour, crisp edges and flat space. [104]

Another artist, Pablo Picasso, similarly embarked on a search towards a modern type. For him this involved focussing on the work of the medieval Catalan painting and African masks, as seen in "Les Demoiselles d'Avingnon" (1907). Although according to some reports, Picasso was working out his own complex and contradictory personal emotional response to women. [105] While retaining what he had learnt from El Greco and Velazquez, Picasso also admired the work of Gauguin and Van Gogh, and possibly indirectly, Japanese prints. His early works demonstrate his willingness to experiment and he was evidently able to assimilate various influences. [106] Gradually the modern painter begins to incorporate other media into the canvass such as Picasso and Braque, who may have been the first to use paper, labels, sawdust, letters and even plaster in their pieces. These were used for the textural qualities and personal expression for suggesting the context of the subject. [107]

The young contemporaries of that day, then, were no longer interested in depicting the illusion of the naturalistic in the academic way as in suggesting light, perspective, space and so forth, but now through experimentation and the technical aspect of painting, treated these areas in different ways. For example, the area of space for a naturalistic painter is solved by the suggestion of the illusion of light from certain directions. The modern painter through experiment began to solve this same problem but through the use of values of colour and large or small bodies. [108] As in the case of Cézanne who opened the door for Cubism. To some extent, then, it may be possible to say that Cézanne, who was first and foremost a painter, opened the way for future artists to paint in a way that later became described as 'painting for its own sake'. [109]

Conclusion

Impressionism, then, by the 1870s connoted a style or technique that was individualistic and taken up by young and old painters alike. This group of individuals having broken all ties with the established salons became totally independent, emerging as painters of modern life desiring to portray the real and the actual as they perceived it in a language appropriate for themselves and which they believed was equivalent to modern times. Their paintings of the urban arena were produced in a new and exciting vein, partly due to the Japanese art that had influenced them and the new city that Haussmann had constructed. So, with the development of a cosmopolitan city came modernity; and coinciding with these changes came a new kind of art depicted by these artists.

With the influx of oriental art came a new and refreshing aesthetics concerning space, perspective, colour, line and composition demonstrated clearly in the work of Degas, Van Gogh and other painters who were seeking to produce paintings of a modern type. There came, therefore, a turning away from the conventionalised subjects prescribed by the academies and a turning inward towards self in their search for expression.

As outlined in Chapter 2, Cézanne also opened a door for exploration, in a sense, for young contemporaries to simply paint – and let paint be paint. Artists then began to research different cultures and other mediums to explore and experiment, enabling them to produce contemporary pieces of work.

In a similar way my own work is based upon observation and at present is keyed into the cosmopolitan arena. My aims in this area are firstly to convey my personal emotional response to the subject through expressive vivacity; allowing paint to be paint. As Degas was particularly focussed on the trivial moment in time, I too pursue a similar line, though for me the focus is on ordinary people in the street, the workers, the people shopping, ladies pushing prams, figures in groups or a single figure who has perhaps caught my attention in some way, and the hustle and bustle of people going to and fro. Although these are the root source and inspiration, the paintings hopefully are portraying movement and life in expressive gestures of the painted surface.

After analysing Degas' work I have begun to incorporate more of a visual language in my work such as truncation and placing a large object or figure close up to the picture plane. The way Van Gogh uses his paint in an expressive manner is exciting in my opinion. He uses paint, it seems, as he feels, and this has been an inspiration to me. For example, Fig 28 attempts to show the hustle and bustle of the busy urban space. The painting is about movement and life. This canvas is quite loose in its application of the paint surface and gives a suggestion of spontaneity, which Degas was well known for. The canvas has been reworked a number of times, not by scraping down, but by adding paint layer upon paint layer so to some extent it has lost its appearance of flux, as compared to Fig 30. In addition to movement and life, the painting intends to convey the idea of a passing moment in time, a moment grasped out of time, so to speak.

Fig 29 is yet another ordinary everyday scene. Here I have used repoussoir, indicated by the railings and foreground post, as well as truncation: the figure on the far left and the two figures cropped by the same post in the middle distance. This painting has not been executed with the spontaneity I would have liked. Instead it has been reworked over a number of occasions. Fig 30 on the other hand is a painting that I am pleased with. It works in the way I intended. It has been reworked but not left to dry before reworking, as in the case of Fig 28 and Fig 29. In this painting I developed the idea of a high viewpoint after Degas and Van Gogh.

Again, it is supposed to convey a moment snatched out of time, but in this instance it was not just an ordinary day, it was a particular event – Wallace and Gromit were in town and people and children were buying balloons. The paint, applied with thick broad brushstrokes of swirls and dashes, some short, some long, is similar to Van Gogh's script and as with the other paintings there is not a great deal of attention paid to detail. This is because the painting is about the movement and life of the subject, portrayed with a variety of expressive marks. Even though this canvas was produced in the studio I aimed at suggesting spontaneity. The final image, Fig 31, is charcoal on paper and is a deliberate attempt to use space as positive space. The major part of the drawing is executed with incised line and other marks including smudging. Finally then, I've been encouraged by the fact that these two artists remained determined to continue in their search for modernity rather than take the same route as those in the academies. In like manner, I am also determined to continue developing my skills as a semi-abstract expressionist fine artist and to stay true to myself.

Illustrations

Fig 1   Woman with Chrysanthemums by Edgar Degas

Fig 2   Beauty with a Letter by Utamaro Kitagowa

Fig 3   The Bellelli Family by Edgar Degas

Fig 4   At the Beach / The Beach Scene by Edgar Degas

Fig 5   Le Déjeuner Sur L'herbe / Luncheon on the Grass by Édouard Manet

Fig 6   Olympia by Édouard Manet

Fig 7   Carlo Pellegrini by Edgar Degas

Fig 8   Horses in a Meadow by Utagawa (Ando) Hiroshige

Fig 9   Race Horses 1866-68 / Jockeys in front of the Grandstand by Edgar Degas

Fig 10 Bolting Horse, by Barry De More after Hokusai, Page 12 from Volume 6 of
The Manga

Fig 11 Napoleon III at the Battle of Solferino by Ernest Meissonier

Fig 12 Pere Tanguy by Vincent Van Gogh

Fig 13 The Ohashi Bridge in the Rain Utagawa (Ando) Hiroshige

Fig 14 Japonaiserie: Oiran / Courtesan by Vincent Van Gogh

Fig 15 Oiran / The Courtesan by Keisai Eisen

Fig 16 The Langlois Bridge with Women Washing by Vincent Van Gogh

Fig 17 The Bedroom by Vincent Van Gogh

Fig 18 The Sower by Vincent Van Gogh

Fig 19 Kintai Bridge / Bridge with Five Arches by Katsushika Hokusai

Fig 20 Moon Pine by Utagawa (Ando) Hiroshige

Fig 21 100 Views of Edo – Haneda Ferry and Beteen Shrine / The Oarsman by
Utagawa (Ando) Hiroshige

Fig 22 La Crau seen from Montmajour by Vincent Van Gogh

Fig 23 Liberty Leading the People by Eugene Delacroix

Fig 24 The Stone Breakers by Gustave Courbet

Fig 25 The Execution of Maximilion by Édouard Manet

Fig 26 A Bar at the Folies-Bérgere by Édouard Manet

Fig 27 The Fifer / Young Flautist by Édouard Manet

Fig 28 Timeless (Street Scene, Bradford) by Barry De More

Fig 29 Woolshops, Halifax by Barry De More

Fig 30 Safe, Secure and Humane by Barry De More

Fig 31 Street Scene, Bradford by Barry De More

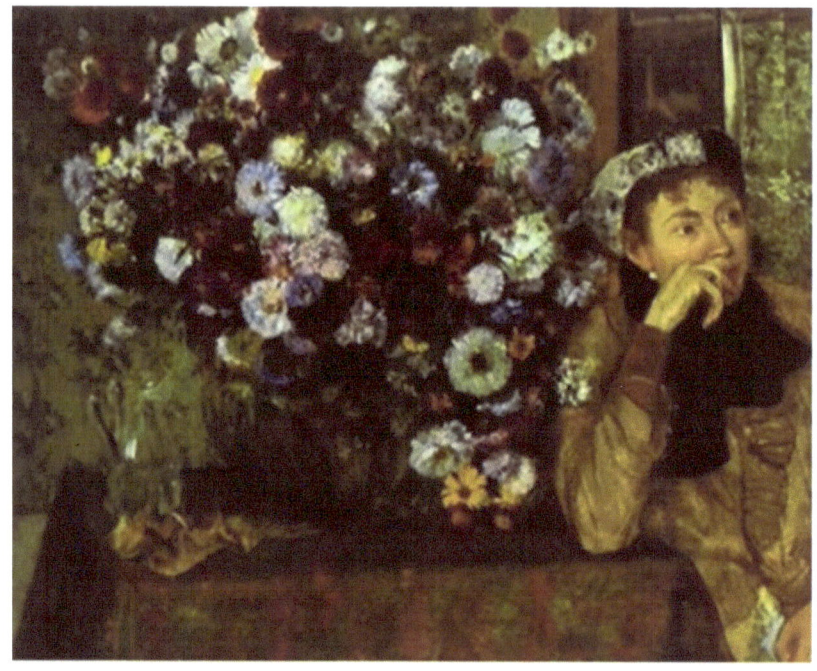

Fig 1   "Woman with Chrysanthemums"

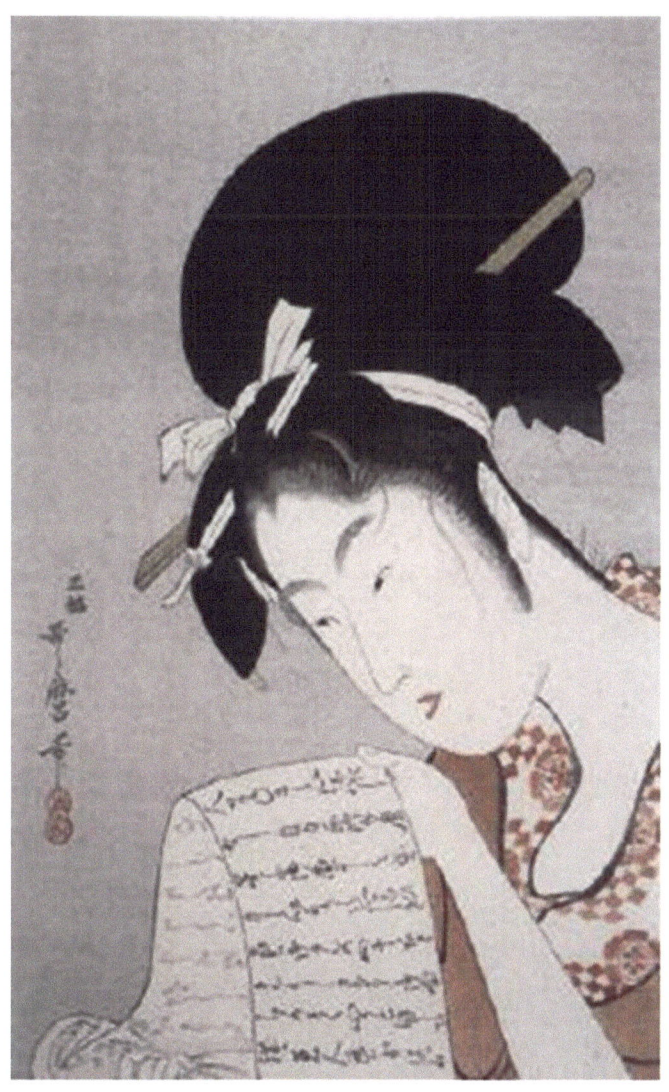

Fig 2 "Beauty with a Letter"

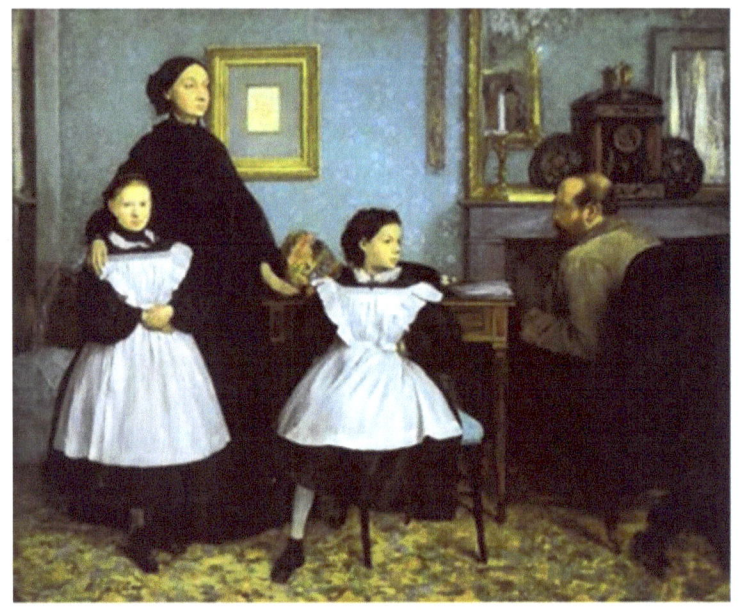

Fig 3   "The Bellelli Family"

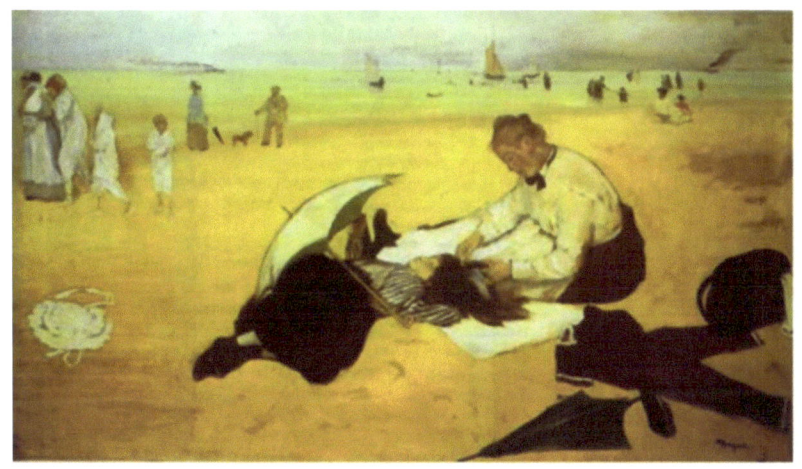

Fig 4   "The Beach Scene" / "At the Beach"

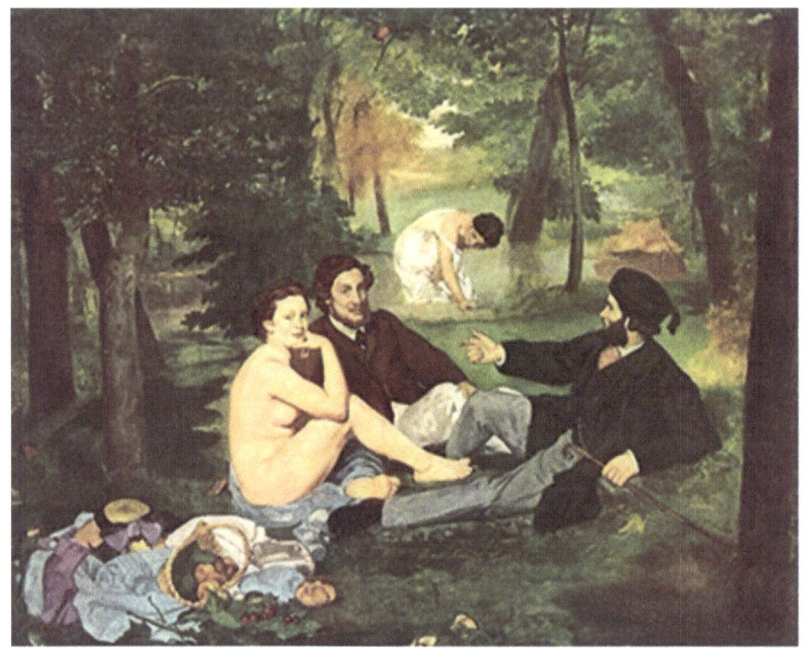

Fig 5   "Le Déjeuner sur L'Herbe" / "Luncheon on the Grass"

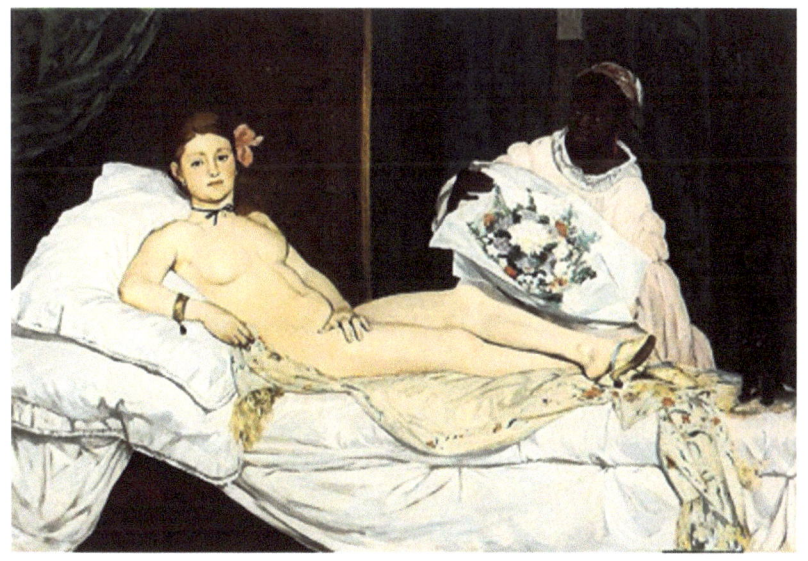

Fig 6   "Olympia"

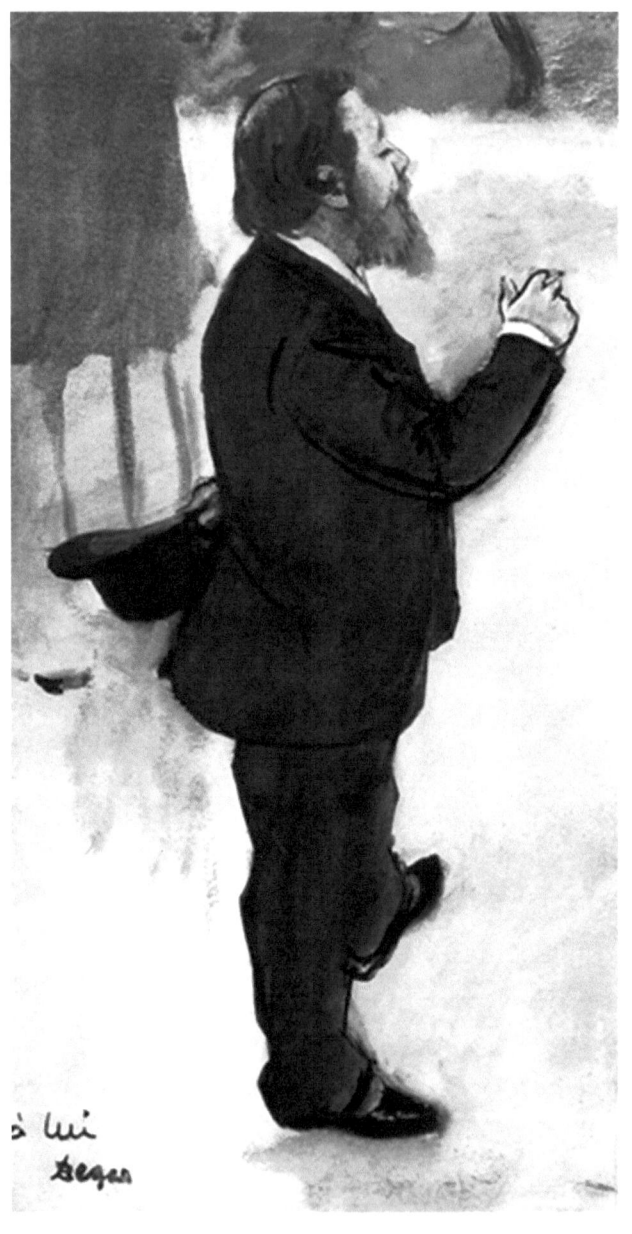

Fig 7   "Carlo Pellegrini"

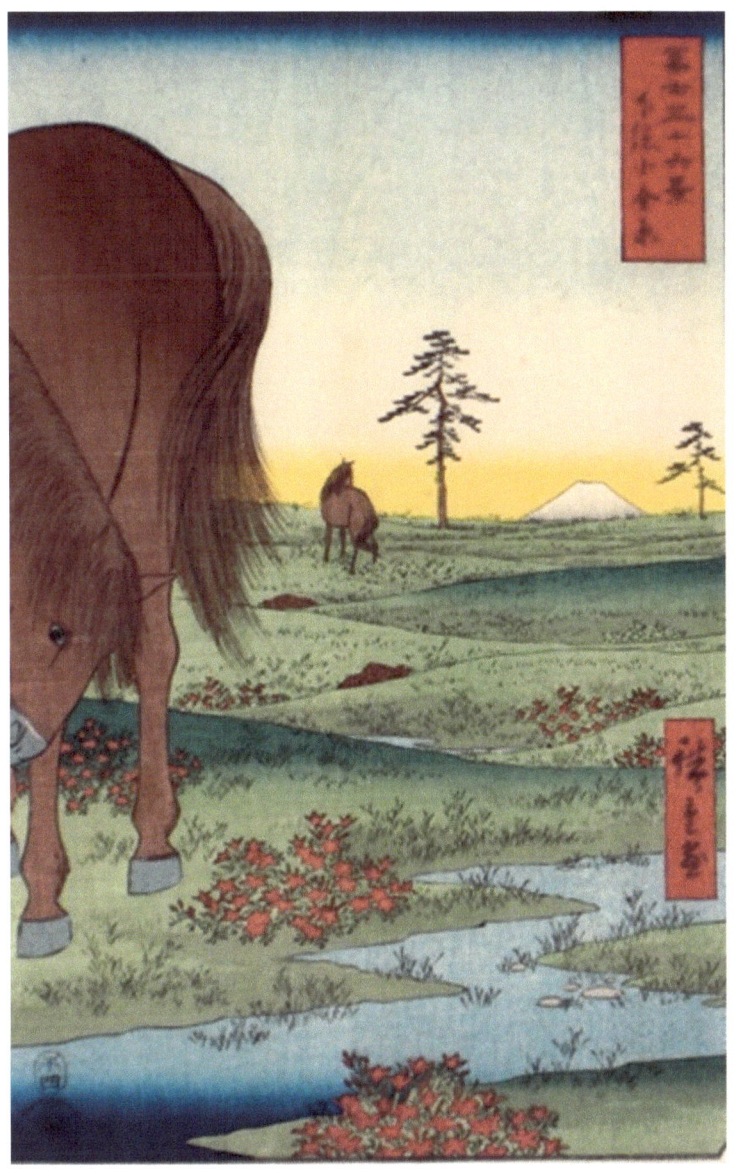

Fig 8　　　　　　　　"Horses in a Meadow"

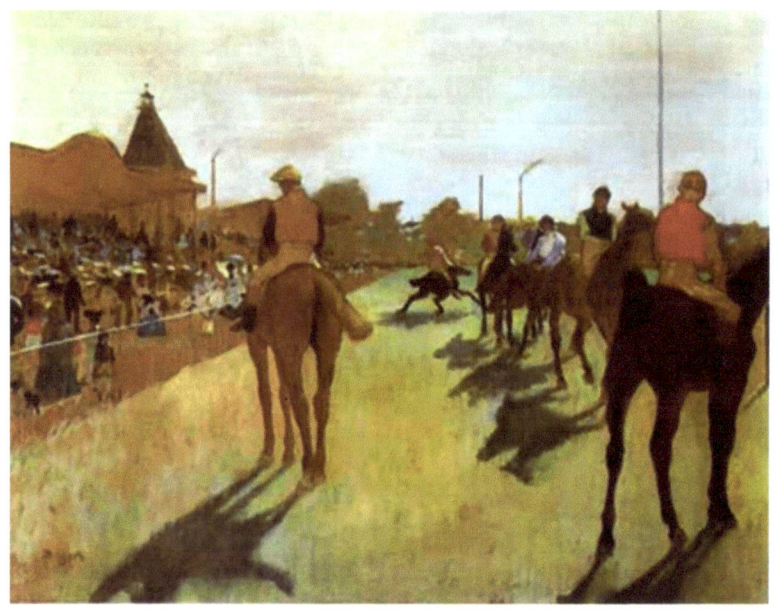

Fig 9   "Race Horses 1866-68" /
              "Jockeys in front of the Grandstand"

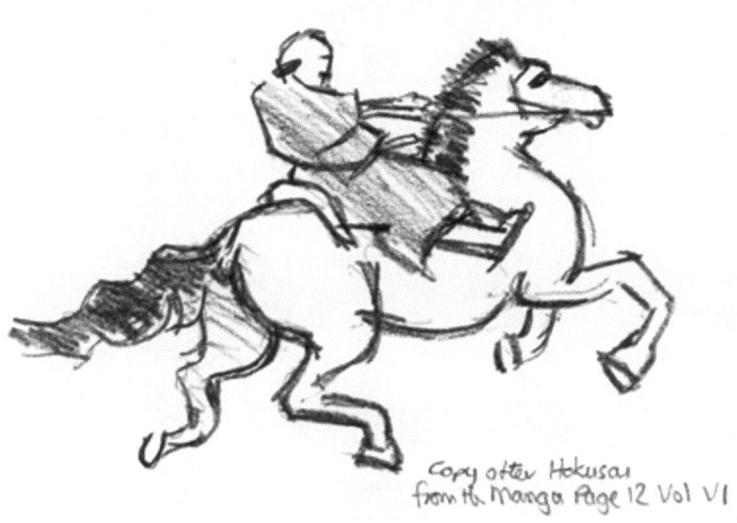

Copy after Hokusai
from the Manga Page 12 Vol VI

Fig 10   "Bolting Horse" by Barry De More
          (After Hokusai, Page 12 from Vol 6 of The Manga)

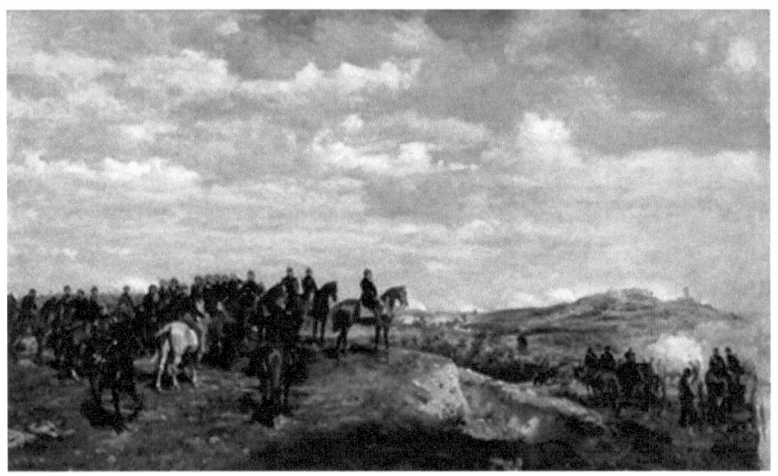

Fig 11   "Napoleon III at the Battle of Solferino"

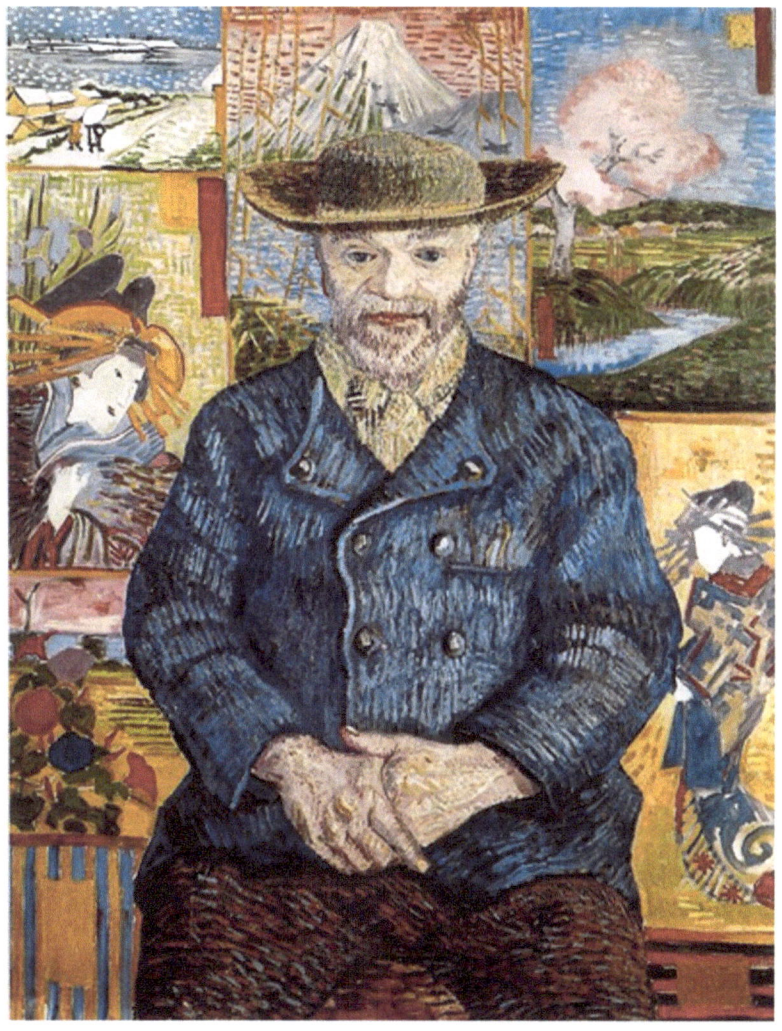

Fig 12   "Pere Tanguy"

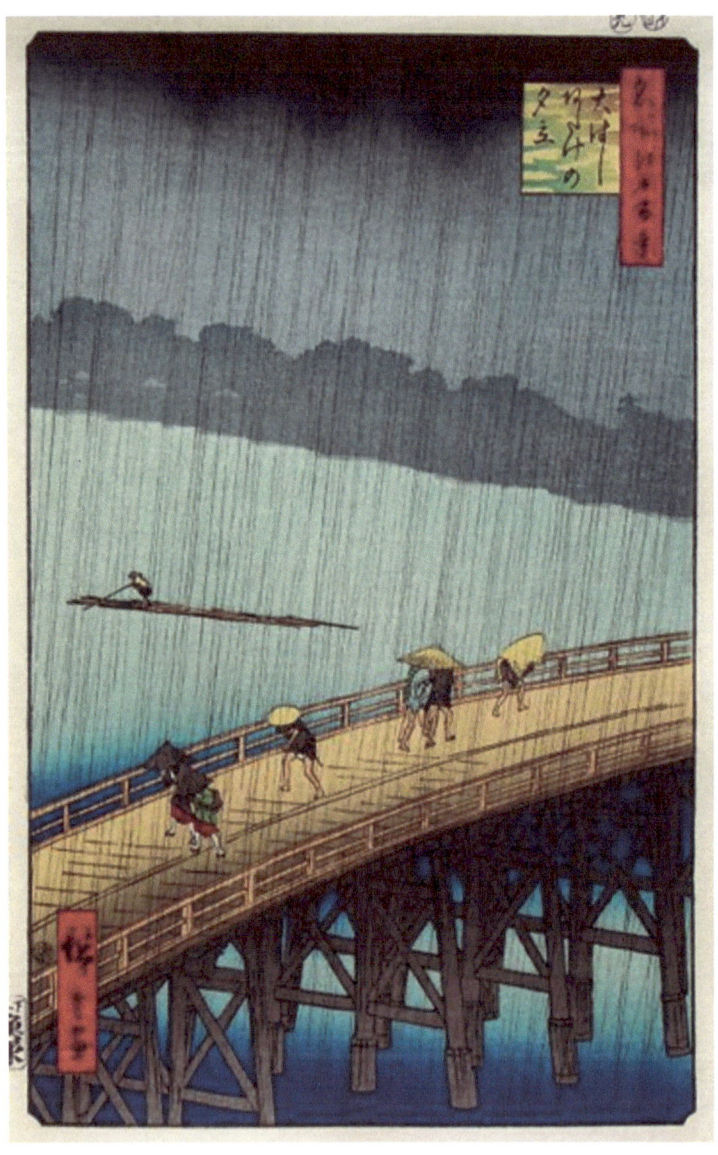

Fig 13   "The Ohashi Bridge in the Rain"

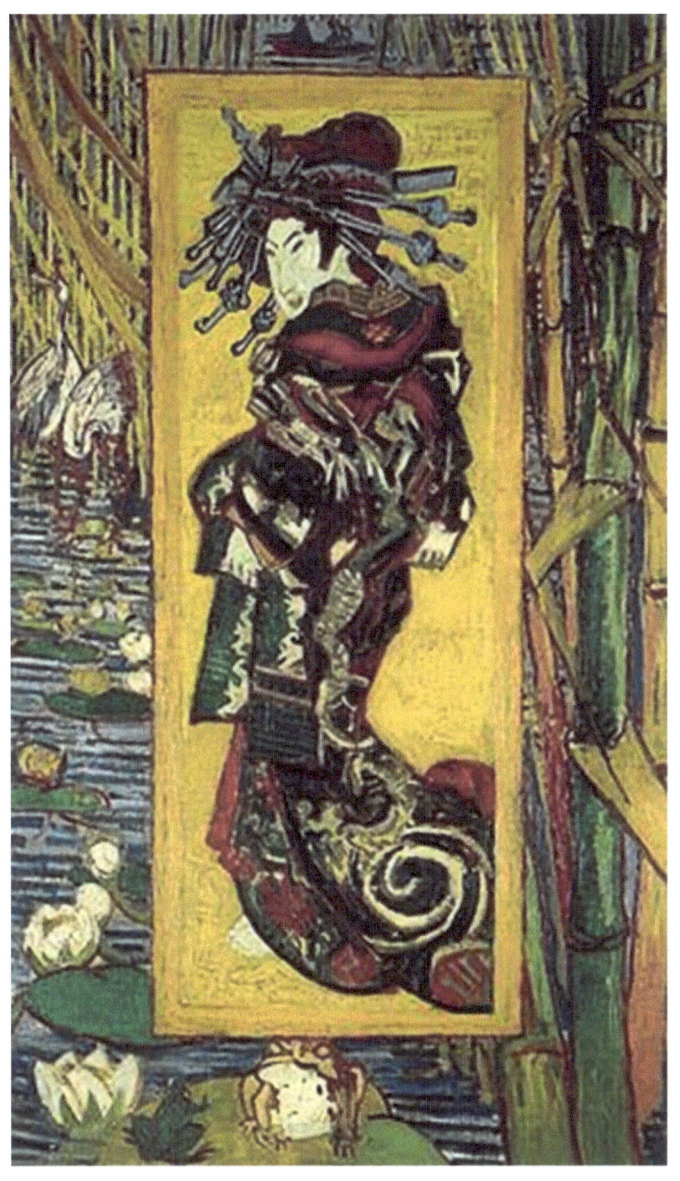

Fig 14   "Japonaiserie: Oiran" / "Courtesan"

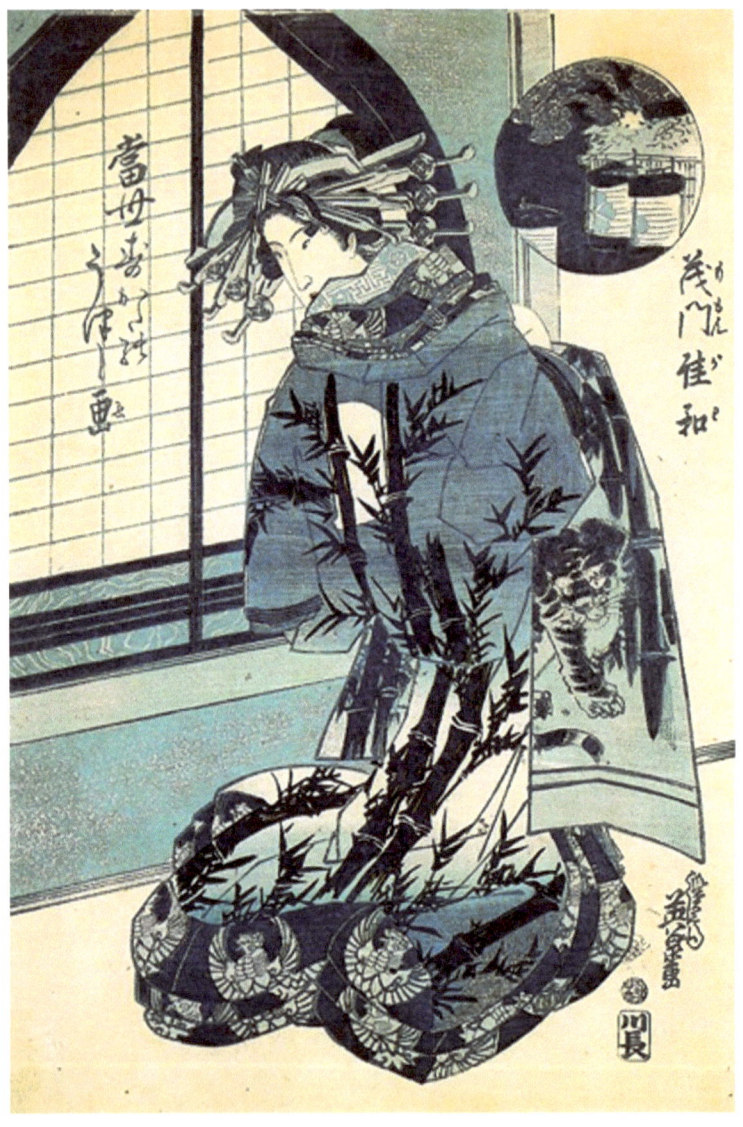

Fig 15   "Oiran" / "The Courtesan"

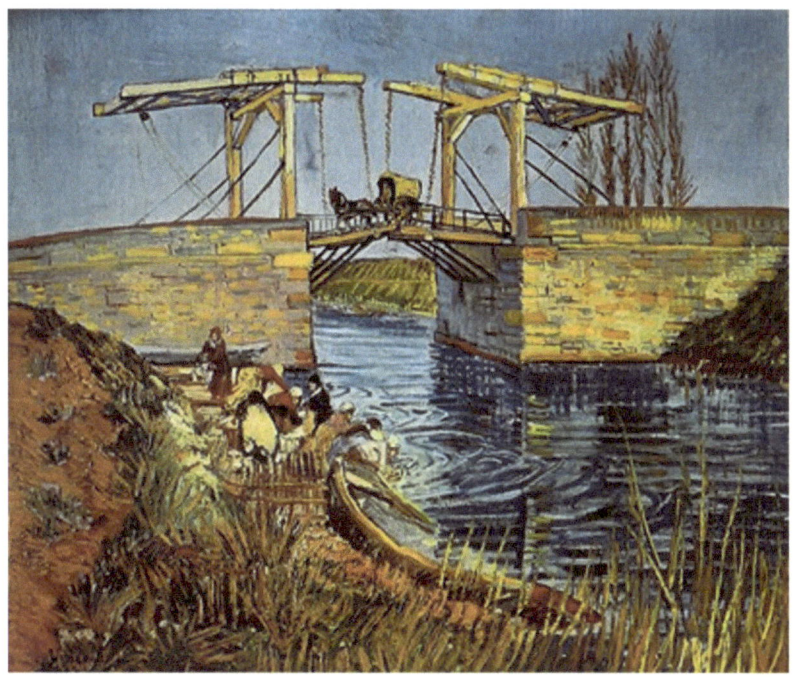

Fig 16   "The Langlois Bridge" / "Women Washing"

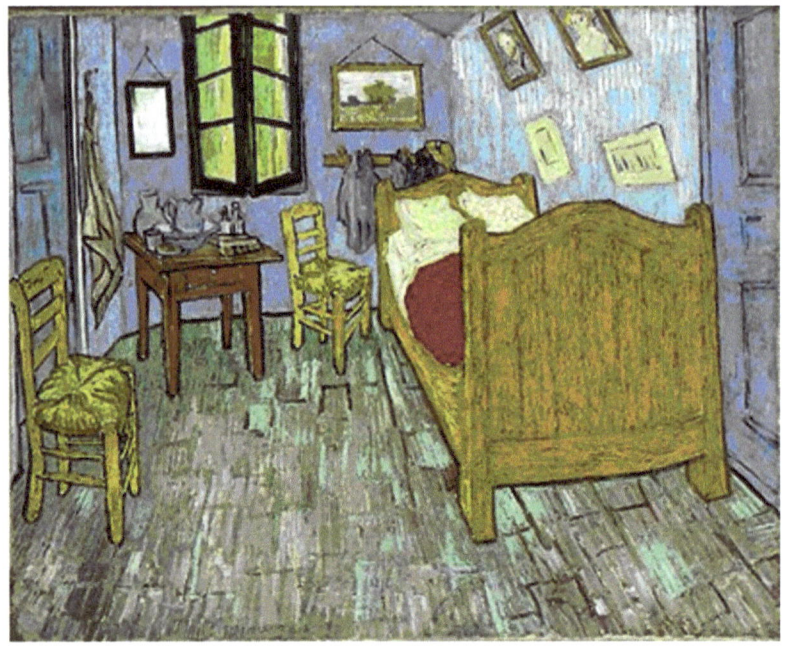

Fig 17   "The Bedroom"

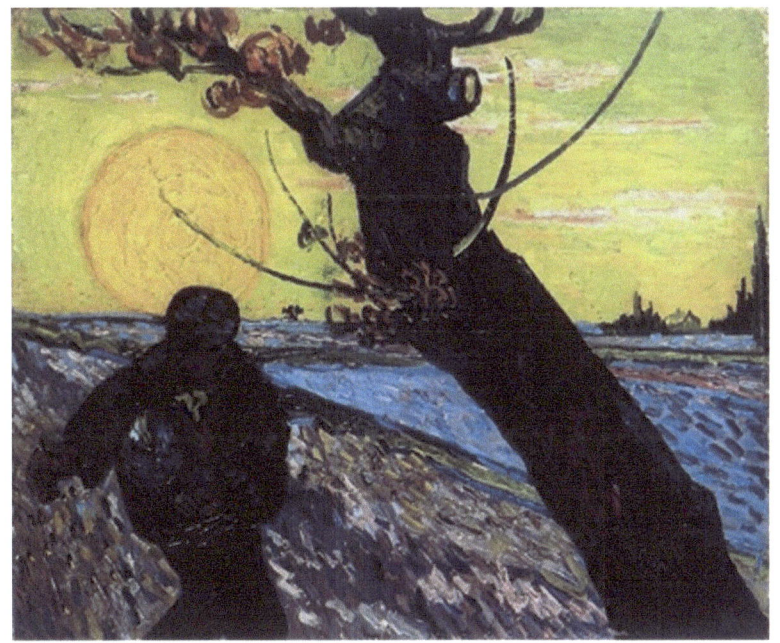

Fig 18   "The Sower"

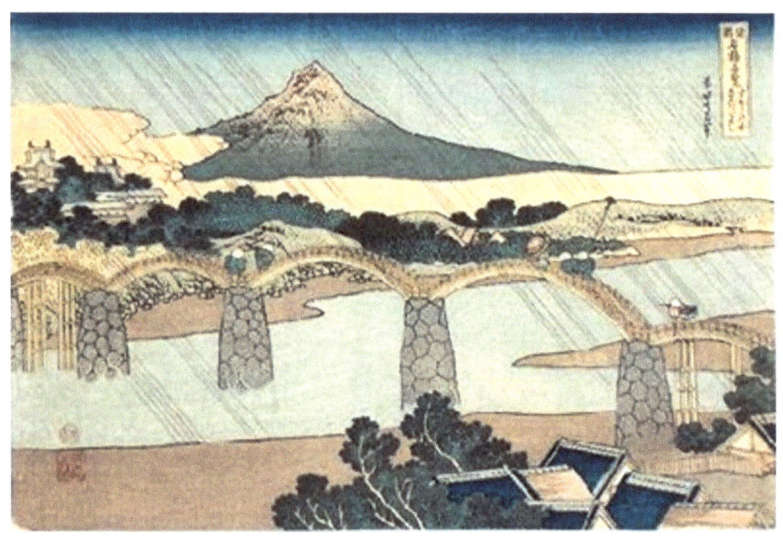

Fig 19   "Kintai Bridge" / "Bridge with Five Arches"

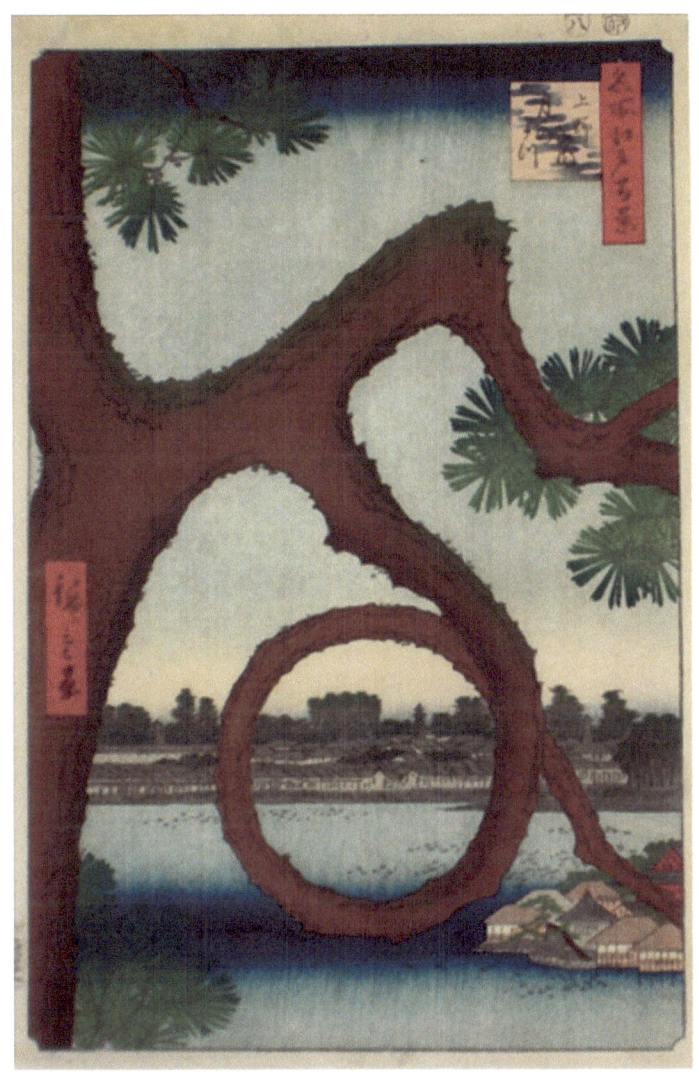

Fig 20   "Moon Pine"

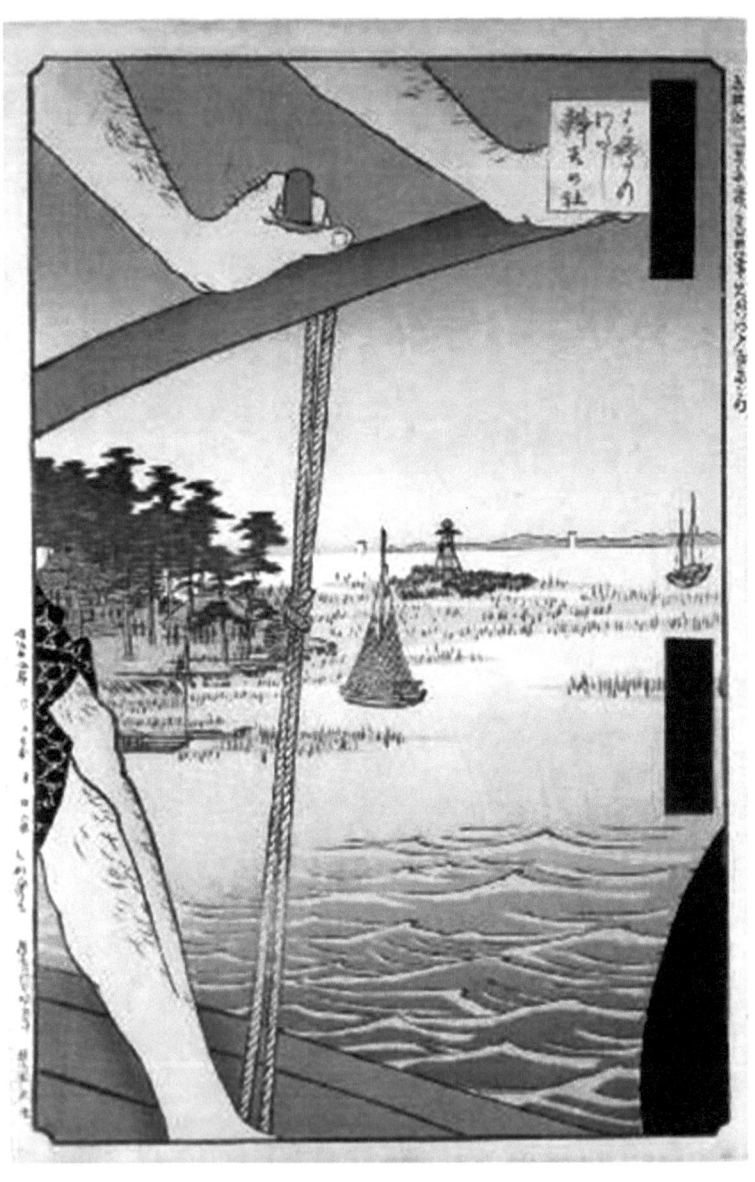

Fig 21 "100 Views of Edo – Haneda Ferry and Beteen Shrine" /
"The Oarsman". Example of repoussoir

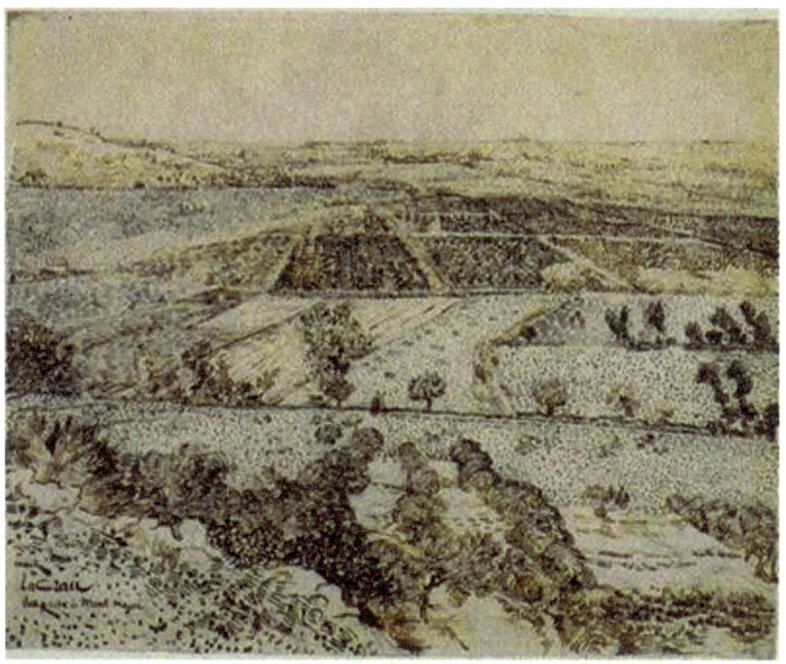

Fig 22   "La Crau seen from Montmajour"

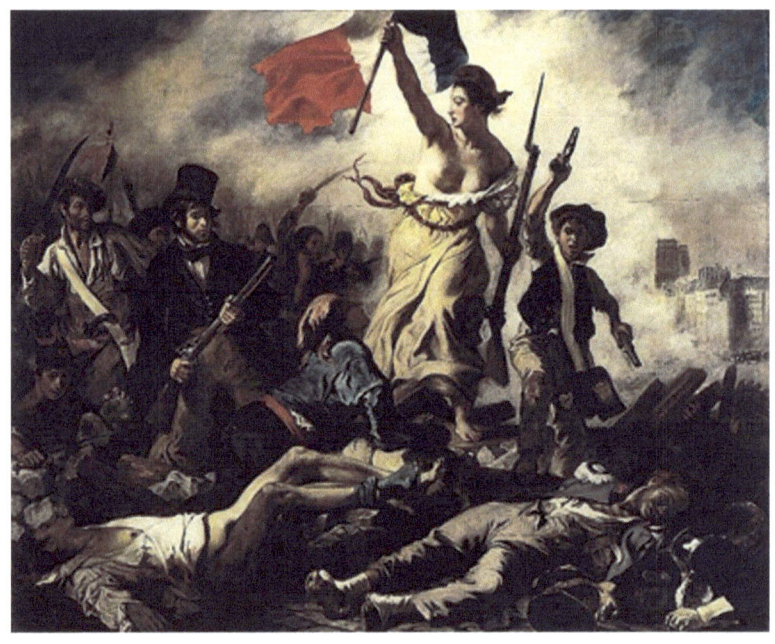

Fig 23   "Liberty Leading the People"

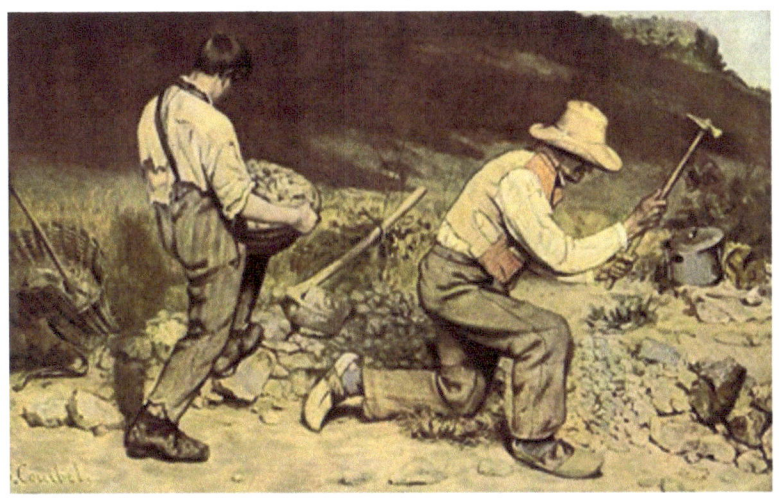

Fig 24   "The Stone Breakers"

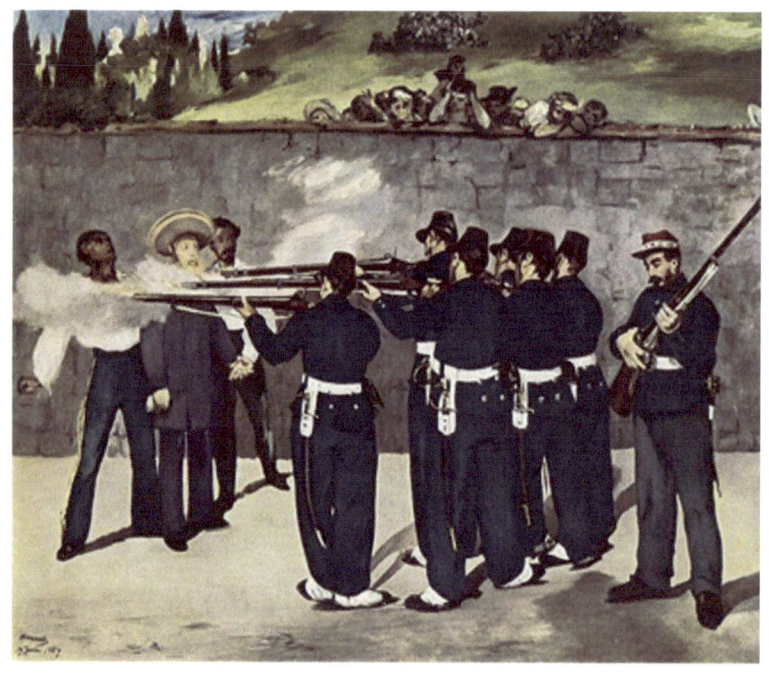

Fig 25   "The Execution of Maximilion

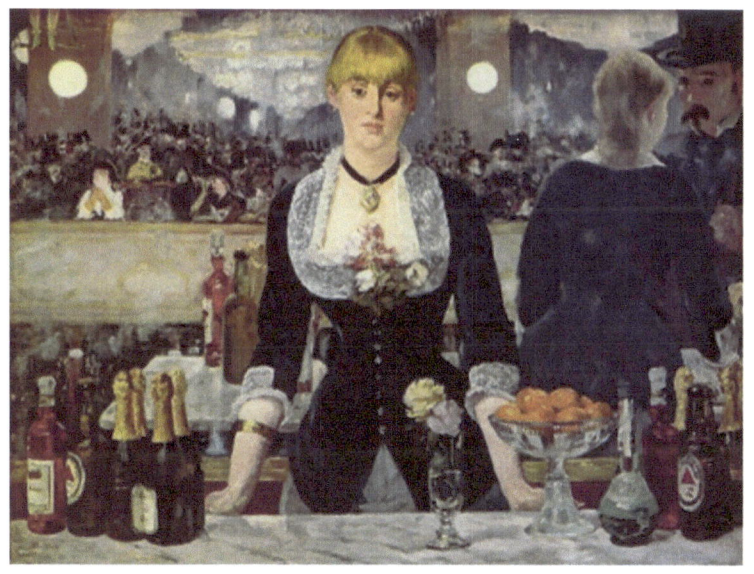

Fig 26   "Bar at the Folies Bergére"

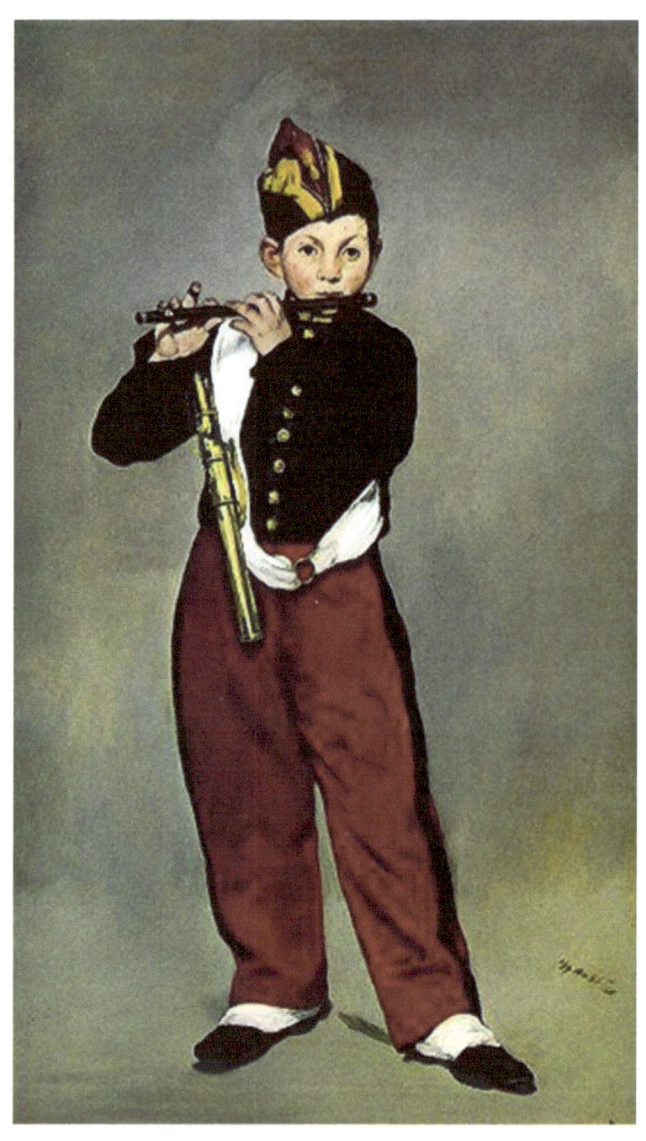

Fig 27   "The Fifer" / "Young Flautist"

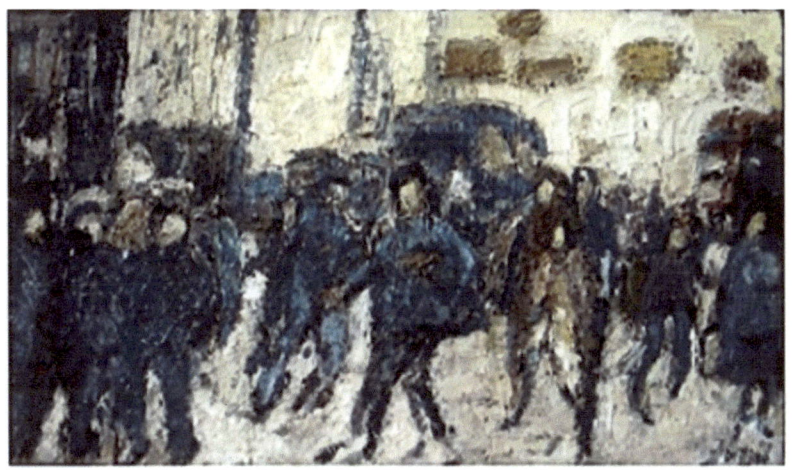

Fig 28   "Timeless" (Bradford Street Scene)

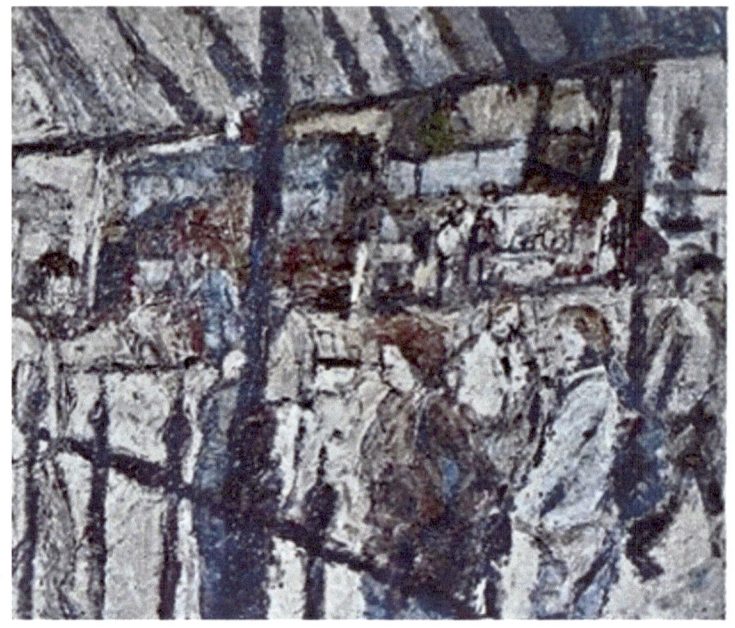

Fig 29   "Woolshops Halifax"

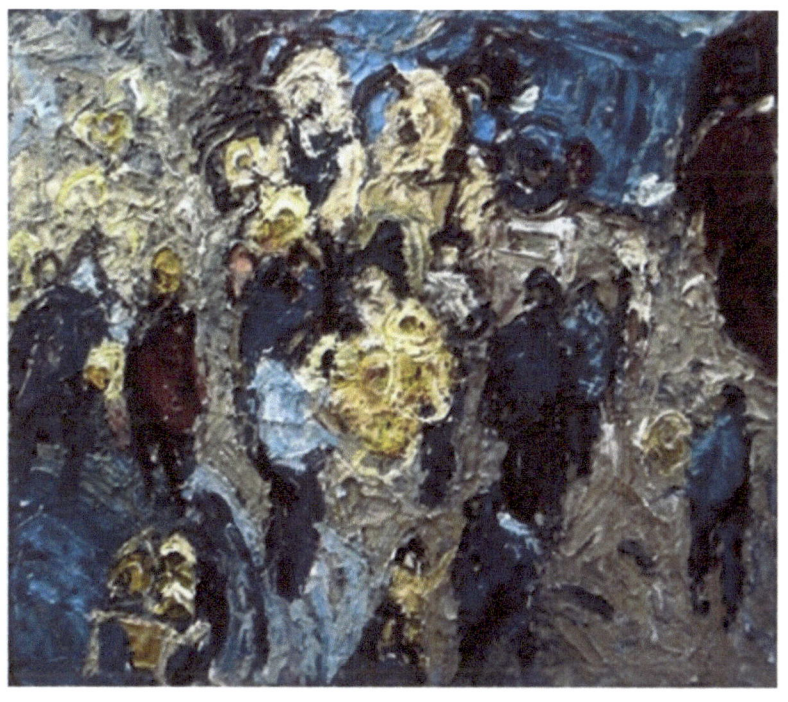

Fig 30   "Safe, Secure and Humane"

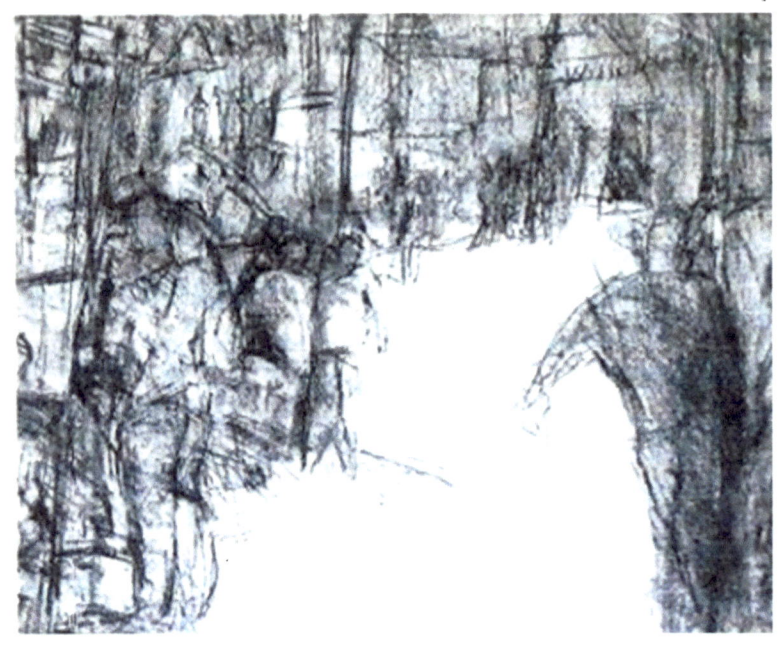

Fig 31   "Street Scene, Bradford"

References

[1] Whitford, F. *Japanese Prints and Western Painters.*
(London: Cassell and Collier MacMillan Publishers Ltd, 1977)
Page 105

[2] Whitford, *Japanese Prints and Western Painters.* Page 105

[3] Flynn, P. (2005) *Visions of People: The Influence of Japanese Prints Ukiyo-e Upon Late Nineteenth and Early Twentieth Century French Art.* [online] Available: http://www.yale.edu [April 2005] Page 6

[4] Herbert, R. *Impressionism, Art, Leisure and Parisian Society*
(London: Guild Publishers by arrangement of Yale University Press, 1989) Page 3

[4a] Pearsall, J. and Trumble, B. (Eds) *Oxford English Reference Dictionary.* 2nd Edition (Oxford: Oxford University Press, 1996)

[5] Flynn, P. [online] Available:
http://www.yale.edu/ynhti/curriculum/units/1982 Page 1 [April 2005]

[6] [online] Available: www.yale.edu Page 1[April 2005]

[7] Whitford, *Japanese Prints and Western Painters.* Page 150

[8] Whitford, *Japanese Prints and Western Painters.* Page 150

[9] Whitford, *Japanese Prints and Western Painters.* Page 150

[10] Whitford, *Japanese Prints and Western Painters.* Page 150

[11] Whitford, *Japanese Prints and Western Painters.* Page 149

[11a] *Édouard Manet's The Races at Longchamps, 1866 and Edgar Degas' Four Studies of a Jockey, 1866* [online] Available:
http://www.artic.edu/artexplorer [July 2005]

[12] Whitford, *Japanese Prints and Western Painters.* Page 104

[13] Whitford, *Japanese Prints and Western Painters.* Page 104

[14] Whitford, *Japanese Prints and Western Painters.* Page 105

[15] Whitford, *Japanese Prints and Western Painters.* Page 161

[16] Whitford, *Japanese Prints and Western Painters.* Page 161

[17] Roberts, K. *Degas.* (London: Phaidon Press Ltd, revised and enlarged edition, 1982) Plate 9

[18] Roberts, K. *Degas,* Plate 12

[19] Whitford, *Japanese Prints and Western Painters.* Page 119

[20] Whitford, *Japanese Prints and Western Painters.* Page 156

[21] Whitford, *Japanese Prints and Western Painters.* Page 155

[22] Roberts, K. *Degas,* Plate 9

[23] Roberts, K. *Degas,* Plate 9

[24] Roberts, K. *Degas,* Page 11

[25] Roberts, K. *Degas,* Page 11

[26] Roberts, K. *Degas,* Page 11

[27] National Gallery of Art, *Courtesan Painting in "Van Gogh's Van Gogh's" inspired by Print in "Edo: Art in Japan* 1615-1868". [online] Available: http://www.nga.gov/press/1998 [April 2005]

[28] [online] Available: http://www.nga.gov/press/1998 [April 2005]

[29] [online] Available: http://www.vangoghmuseum.com/research/library page 4 [June 2005]

[30] Author anonymous [online] Available: http://www.dominopatrici.com *The Impact of Japanese Woodblock Prints on Impressionism during the Mid-Nineteenth to Late-Nineteenth Century.* [November 2005]

[31] [online] Available: http://www.vangoghmuseum.com/permenantcollection/Paris1886 -87 page 1 [June 2005]

[32] [online] Available:
http://www.vangoghmuseum.com/permenantcollection/Paris1886
-87 page 2 [June 2005]

[33] Elgar, F. *Van Gogh, A Study of his Life and* Works (London: Thames and Hudson, 1966) Page 106

[34] Elgar, *Van Gogh, A Study of his Life and Work.* Page 106

[35] Whitford, *Japanese Prints and Western Painters.* Page 193

[36] Elgar, *Van Gogh, A Study of his Life and Works.* Page 89

[37] [online] Available:
http://www.vangoghmuseum.com/permanentcollection page 1
[June 2005]

[38] Walter, I. F. and Metzger, R. Translated by Hulse, M. *Vincent Van Gogh, The Complete Paintings* (Koln, Germany: Benedickt Tachen Verlag Publishers, 1993) Page 323

[39] Walter and Metzger, *Vincent Van Gogh, The Complete Paintings,* Page 323-325

[40] Walter and Metzger, *Vincent Van Gogh, The Complete Paintings,* Page 325

[41] Walter and Metzger, *Vincent Van Gogh, The Complete Paintings,* Page 325

[42] Dunlop, I. *Van Gogh, Great Lives* (London: George Weidenfeld and Nicolson Ltd, 1974) Page 155

[43] Walter and Metzger, Vincent Van Gogh, The Complete Paintings, Page 345

[44] [online] Available:
http://www.vangoghmuseum.com/permanentcollectionseeing colour Page 2 [June 2005]

[45] *Repoussoir.* [online] Available:
http://www.aol.oxfordreference.com/views/ENTRY [March 2006]

[46] Author anonymous. *Vincent Van Gogh.* [online] Available: http://www.arthive.com/v/van-gogh/sower/text [March 2006]

[47] Whitford, *Japanese Prints and Western Painters.* Page 193 and Page 197

[48] Whitford, *Japanese Prints and Western Painters.* Page 193 and 197

[49] Goblik, S. *Has Modernism Failed?* London: Thames and Hudson (1984) page 24

[50] Witco, C. *Roots of Modernism.* [online] Available: http://www.arthistory.sbc.edu Page 3 [December 2005]

[51] [online] Available: http://www.arthistory.sbc.edu *Roots of Modernism.* Page 3

[52] [online] Available: http://www.arthistory.sbc.edu *Roots of Modernism*

[53] [online] Available: http://www.arthistory.sbc.edu *Roots of Modernism*

[54] Available from http://www.arthistory.sbc.edu *Roots of Modernism,* Page 8

[55] Available from http://www.arthistory.sbc.edu *Roots of Modernism,* Page 8

[56] [online] Available: http://www.arthistory.sbc.edu Witco, C. *Art For Art's Sake.* Page 2

[57] [online] Available: http://www.arthistory.sbc.edu Witco, C. *Art For Art's Sake.* Page 9

[58] [online] Available: http://www.arthistory.sbc.edu Witco, C. *Art For Art's Sake.* Page 3

[59] Author anonymous. *Modernism.* [online] Available: http://www.wikipedia.org Page 1 [December 2005]

[60] [online] Available: http://www.wikipedia.org *Modernism.* Page 1

[61] [online] Available: http://www.wikipedia.org *Modernism.* Page 1

[62] [online] Available: http://www.wikipedia.org *Modernism.* Page 2

[63] [online] Available: http://www.wikipedia.org *Modernism.* Page 1

[64] Author anonymous. *Vincent Van Gogh.* [online] Available: http://www.sparknotes.com Page 2 [December 2005]

[64a] Pearsall, J. and Trumble, B. (Eds) *Oxford English Reference Dictionary.* 2nd Edition (Oxford: Oxford University Press, 1996)

[65] Author anonymous. *Breaking Away from the Academy.* [online] Available: http://www.gallery.sisu.edu [December 2005]

[66] As above

[67] As above

[68] [online] Available: http://www.wikipedia.org *A Bar at the Folies-Bergere.*

[69] As above

[70] [online] Available: http://www.gallery.sisu.edu *Breaking Away from the Academy, Influence of Photo.* [December 2005]

[71] [online] Available: http://www.gallery.sisu.edu *Japanese Influence. Introduction.* [June 2005]

[72] [online] Available: http://www.dominopatrici.com/art/history [November 2005]

[73] [online] Available: http://www.dominopatrici.com/art/history

[74] [online] Available: http://ww.dominopatrici.com/art/history

[75] [online] Available: http://ww.dominopatrici.com/art/history

[76] [online] Available: http://www.artlex.com Page 6 [April 2005]

[77] [online] Available: http://www.dominopatrici.com Page 2

[78] [online] Available: http://www.geocities.com Page 1 [2005]

[79] [online] Available: http://www.geocities.com page 1

[80] [online] Available: http://www.geocities.com

[81] [online] Available: http://www.geocities.com

[82] Krikke, J. *China, Japan and the Birth of Modernism.* Page 2 [online] Available: http://www.home.uni.one [December 2005]

[83] Krikke, J. Page 2 [online] Available: http://www.home.uni.one

[84] Krikke, J. Page 2 [online] Available: http://www.home.uni.one

[85] Krikke, J. Page 2 [online] Available: http://www.home.uni.one

[86] Krikke, J. Page 3 [online] Available: http://www.home.uni.one

[87] Greenburg, C. *Modernist Painting.* Page 1 and 6. In: 'Modern Art and Modernism. A Critical Anthology.' Frascina, F., Harrison, C. and Paul. D. (Eds)(London: Harper and Row Publishers. 1982)

[88] Greenburg, C. *Modernist Painting.* Page 6

[89] Greenburg, C. *Modernist Painting.* Page 6

[90] Kendall, R. *Cézanne by Himself.* (London: Guild Publishing. 1988) Page 8

[91] Kendall, R. *Cézanne by Himself.* Page 10

[92] Kendall, R. *Cézanne by Himself.* Page 11

[93] Kendall, R. *Cézanne by Himself.* Page 11

[94] Kendall, R. *Cézanne by Himself.* Page 8

[95] Greenburg, C. *Modernist Painting.* Page 6

[96] Greenburg, C. *Modernist Painting.* Page 6

[97] Greenburg, C. *Modernist Painting.* Page 7

[98] Greenburg, C. *Modernist Painting.* Page 7

[99] Greenburg, C. *Modernist Painting.* Page 7

[100] Greenburg, C. *Modernist Painting*. Page 9

[101] Denis, M. *From Gauguin and Van Gogh to Classicism*. In: 'Modern Art and Modernism. A Critical Anthology' Frascina, F. and Harrison, C. (Eds) (London: Harper and Row Publishers. 1982) Page 51

[102] Fry, R. *The French Post-Impressionists*. In: 'Modern Art and Modernism. A Critical Anthology' Frascina, F. and Harrison, C (Eds) (London: Harper and Row Publishers. 1982) Page 89

[103] Fry, R. *The French Post-Impressionists*. Page 90

[104] Copplestone, T. *Modern Art*. (London: The Hamlyn Publishing Group.1985) Page 51

[105] Copplestone, T. *Modern Art*. Page 52

[106] Read, H. *Art and Artists*. (London: Thames and Hudson. 1994) Page 276

[107] Tarabukin, N. *From the Easel to the Machine*. In: 'Modern Art and Modernism, A Critical Anthology'. Frascina, F. and Harrison, C. (Eds) (London: Harper and Row Publishers. 1982) Page 137

[108] Tarabukin, N. *From the Easel to the Machine*. Page 136

[109] Bernard, E. (1868-1941) *Paul Cézanne*. In: 'Art in Theory 1815-1900. An Anthology of Changing Ideas.' Harrison, C., Wood, F. and Gaiger, J. (Eds)(Oxford: Blackwell Publishers Ltd. 1998) Page 986

Bibliography

Texts

Anderson, J. *The Art of the Impressionists.* (Great Britain: Parragon Book Service Ltd, 1994)

Bernard, B. *Vincent by Himself* (London: Book Club Associates by Arrangement with Macdonald & Co Ltd, 1986) Copplestone, T. *Modern Art* (London: Hamlyn Publishing, 1985)

Copplestone, T. *Modern Art.* (London: The Hamlyn Publishing Group. 1985

Denis, M. *From Gauguin and Van Gogh to Classicism.* In: 'Modern Art and Modernism. A Critical Anthology' Frascina, F. and Harrison, C. (Eds) (London: Harper and Row Publishers. 1982) Page 51

Dunlop, I. *Van Gogh, Great Lives* (London: George Weidenfeld and Nicolson Ltd, 1974)

Elgar, F. *Van Gogh A Study Of His Life And Work* (London: Thames and Hudson, 1966)

Fry, R. *The French Post-Impressionists.* In: 'Modern Art and Modernism. A Critical Anthology' Frascina, F. and Harrison, C. (Eds) (London: Harper and Row Publishers. 1982)

Gibson, S.R. *A Handbook of Modern History World History since 1870* (New York: Longman Group Ltd, 1986)

Goblik, S. *Has Modernism Failed?* London: Thames and Hudson (1984)

Greenburg, C. *Modernist Painting.* Page 1 and 6. In: 'Modern Art and Modernism. A Critical Anthology.' Frascina, F., Harrison, C. and Paul. D. (Eds) (London: Harper and Row Publishers. 1982)

Herbert, R. *Impressionism, Art, Leisure & Parisian Society* (London: Guild Publishers by arrangement of Yale University Press, 1989)

Kendall, R. *Degas By Himself, Drawings, Prints, Paintings, Writing* (London: Time Warner Books UK, 2004)

Lucie-Smith, E. *Lives of the Great Twentieth Century Artists* (London: Weidenfeld and Nicolson, 1986)

Marceau, Jo (Ed) *Art A World History* (London: Darling Kindersley Ltd, 2002)

Pearsall, J. and Trumble, B. (Eds) *Oxford English Reference Dictionary.* 2nd Edition (Oxford: Oxford University Press, 1996)

Read, H. *Art and Artists.* (London: Thames and Hudson. 1994)

Roberts, K. *Degas.* (London: Phaidon Press Ltd, revised and enlarged edition, 1982)

S.A.I.E. *Modern French Masters. The Impressionists* (London: Bloomsbury Books, 1989)

Stangos, N. and Read, H. (Eds) *Dictionary of Art and Artists* (London: Thames and Hudson, 1994)

Tarabukin, N. *From the Easel to the Machine.* In: 'Modern Art and Modernism, A Critical Anthology'. Frascina, F. and Harrison, C. (Eds) (London: Harper and Row Publishers. 1982)

Thompson, R. *The Private Degas* (London: Arts Council of Great Britain and The Herbert Press Ltd, 1987)

Tralbaut, M. E. *Van Gogh A Pictorial Biography* (London: Thames and Hudson, 1959)

Wallace, R. *The World of Van Gogh* (USA: Time Inc., 1972)

Walther, I. F. and Metzger, R. Translated by Hulse, M. *Vincent Van Gogh The Complete Paintings* (Koln, Germany: Benedickt Tachen Verlag Publishers, 1993)

Whitford, F. *Japanese Prints and Western Painters* (London: Cassell and Collier Macmillan Publishers Ltd, 1977

Electronic Sources

Art Institute of Chicago. *Edgar Degas' Yellow Dancers (In the Wings),* 1874/76.
[online] Available: http://www.artic.edulartexplorer/search [July 2005]

Art Institute of Chicago. *Édouard Manet's The Races at Longchamps,* 1866 *and Edgar Degas ' Four Studies of a Jockey,* 1866. [online] Available: http://www.artic.edulartexplorer/search [July 2005]

Author anonymous. *About Vincent Van Gogh.* [online] Available: http://www.artlex.com [April 2005]

Author anonymous. *Breaking Away from the Academy.* [online] Available: http://www.gallery.sisu.edu [December 2005]

Author anonymous. *Degas, Edgar.* [online] Available: http://www.encarter.msn.com/encyclopedia [April 2005]

Author anonymous. *Edgar Degas,* 1834-1917, *Biography.* [online] Available: http://www.expodegas.com [April 2005]

Author anonymous. *Emile Zola (1840-1902).* [online] Available: http://www.kiriasto.sci.fi [June 2005]

Author anonymous. *Famous Paintings.* [online] Available: http://www.van-gogh-art.co.uk [June 2005]

Author anonymous. *France 1870-1890: Domestic Policy.* [online] Available: http://www.zum.de/whkmla/region/France [April 2005]

Author anonymous. *France 1870-1890: Intellectual Life.* [online] Available: http://www.zum.de/whkmla/regionIFrance [April 2005]

Author anonymous. *France 1870-1890: The Economy.* [online] Available: http://www.zum.de/whkmla/region/France [April 2005]

Author anonymous. *Hiroshige* (1797-1858). [online] Available: http://www.secutor.se/Ukiyo-e [June 2005]

Author anonymous. *Hokusai and Japanese Art.*[online] Available:

http://www.andreas.com/hokusai.html [July 2005]

Author anonymous. *Impressionism - Biography of Edgar Degas.* [online] Available: http://www.Impressioniste.net/degas-edgar.htm [July 2005]

Author anonymous. *Ingres, Jean-Auguste-Dominique.* [online] Available: http://www.ibiblio.org/wm/paint/auth/ingres [April 2005]

Author anonymous. *Japanese Prints.* [online] Available: http://www.artelino.com/forum/articlesindex.asp [April 2005]

Author anonymous. *Japanese Prints General Notes.* [online] Available: http://www.vam.ac.uk [June 2005]

Author anonymous. *Modernism.* [online] Available: http://www.wikipedia.org Page 1 [December 2005]

Author anonymous. *Paris Commune 1870-1871.* [online] Available: http://www.zum.de/whkmla/region/France [April 2005]

Author anonymous. *Paul Eugene Henri Gauguin (1848-1903).* [online] Available: http://www.vangogh-art.co.uk [June 2005]

Author anonymous. *Roots of Modernism.* Page 3[online] Available: http://www.arthistory.sbc.edu

Author anonymous. *10 of Vincent Letters and Sketches.* [online] Available: http://www.van-gogh-art.co.uk [June 2005]

Author anonymous. *The Impact of Japanese Woodblock Prints on Impressionism during the Mid-Nineteenth to Late-Nineteenth Century* [online] Available: http://www.dominopatrici.com [November 2005]

Author anonymous. *Ukiyo-e.* [online] Available: http://www.artelino.com/articles/ukivo-e.asp [April 2005]

Author anonymous. *Ukiyo-e ("Pictures of the Floating World").* [online] Available: http://www.artelino.com/articles/ukivo-e.asp [April 2005]

Author anonymous. *Utagawa Hiroshige Masterpieces, Plum Orchard* [online]

Available: http://www.riikmuseum.nl/aria/aria-dictionarv/Ukiyo-e [June 2005]

Author anonymous. *Van Gogh and Japonisme.* [online] Available: http://www.artelino.com/articles/van goghjaponisme.asp [June 2005]

Author anonymous. *Van Gogh Museum: Van Gogh's Literary Sources* [online] Available: http://www.vangoghmuseum.nl/bisrd [June 2005]

Author anonymous. *Van Gogh Museum* 1886-1887, *Permanent Collection, Paris 1886-1887* [online] Available: http://www.vangoghmuseum.nl/bisrd [June 2005]

Author anonymous. *Van Gogh Museum* 1888, *Permanent Collection, Arles* 1888. [online] Available: http://www.vangoghmuseum.nl/bisrd [June 2005]

Author anonymous. *Van Gogh Museum* 1889, *Permanent Collection, Saint-Remy 1889.* [online] Available: http://www.vangoghmuseum.nl/bisrd [June 2005]

Author anonymous. *Vincent Van Gogh.* [online] Available: http://www.arthive.com/v/van-gogh/sower/text [March 2006]

Author anonymous. *Vincent Van Gogh.* [online] Available: http://www.sparknotes.com page 2 [December 2005]

Author anonymous. *Vincent Van Gogh (1853-1890).* [online] Available: http://www.metmuseum.org [June 2005]

Author anonymous. *Vincent Van Gogh (1853-1890) Biography.*[online] Available: http://www.expo-shop.com [July 2005]

Author anonymous. *Vincent Van Gogh (1853-1890).* [online] Available: http://www.metmuseum.org/toah [April 2005]

Boyle, D. *Edgar Degas Biography* 1834-1917.   [online] Available: http://www.artelino.com/articles/edgar-degas.asp [April 2005]

Constantin, S. *Van Gogh Museum: Technical and Conservation Research.* [online] Available: http://www.vangoghmuseum.com [June 2005]

Florillo, J (2001) *Viewing Japanese Prints: Attribution of Hokusai's Kachoe-e.*
[online] Available: http://www.spectacle.berkeley.edu [June 2005]

Florillo, J (2001) *Viewing Japanese Prints: Katsushika Hokusai (1760-1849)*
[online] Available: http://www.spectacle.berkeley.edu [June 2005]

Florillo, J (2001) *Viewing Japanese Prints: Keisai Eisen (1790-1848).*
[online] Available: http://www.spectacle.berkeley.edu [June 2005]

Florillo, J (2001) *Viewing Japanese Prints: Mu Tamagawa (Six Jewel Rivers)* [online] Available: http://www.spectacle.berkeley.edu [June 2005]

Florillo, J (2004) *Viewing Japanese Prints: Ukiyo-e ("Pictures of the Floating World".* [online] Available: http://www.spectacle.berkeley.edu [June 2005]

Flynn, P. *Visions of People: The Influence Of Japanese Prints Ukiyo-e Upon Late Nineteenth and Early Twentieth Century French Art* [online] Available:
http://www.yale.edu/vnhti/curriculum/units/1982 [April 2005]

Krikke, J. *China, Japan and the Birth of Modernism.* Page 2 [online] Available: http://www.home.uni.one [December 2005]

Ives, C. *Japonisme.* [online] Available: http://www.metmuseum.org [June 2005]

National Gallery of Art, *Courtesan Painting in "Van Gogh's Van Goghs" inspired by Print in "Edo: Art in Japan* 1615-1868". [online] Available: http://www.nga.gov/press/1998 [April 2005]

Pioch, N (2002) *Degas, Edgar: Woman Combing her Hair.* [online] Available: http://www.ibiblio.org/wm/paint/auth/degas [April 2005]

Repoussoir. [online] Available:
http://www.aol.oxfordreference.com/views/ENTRY [March 2006]

Samu, M. *Impressionism: Art and Modernity.* [online] Available:
http://www.metmuseum.org [June 2005]

Stephens, P. *Japanese Influences upon Vincent Van Gogh*
[online] Available: http://www.art.unt.edu [April 2005]

Stewart, B. *A Guide to Japanese Prints. Chapter XIX*
The Hundred Famous Views of Yedo [online] Available:
http://www.hiroshige.org.uk/hiroshige.stewart [June 2005]

Voorhies, J. *Post-Impressionism.* [online] Available:
http://www.metmuseum.org [June 2005]

Webmuseum, *Paris Degas, Edgar. Ballet Dancers.* [online] Available:
http://www.ibiblio.org/wmpaint/auth/degas/ballet [April 2005]

www.ingramcontent.com/pod-product-compliance
Lightning Source LLC
Chambersburg PA
CBHW040814200526
45159CB00024B/2933